IN FOCUS

GUATEMALA

A Guide to the People, Politics and Culture

Trish O'Kane

LATIN AMERICA BUREAU

INTERLINK BOOKS
NEW YORK

First published in 2000

In the U.S.:

Interlink Books
An imprint of Interlink Publishing Group, Inc.
99 Seventh Avenue, Brooklyn, New York 11215

Library of Congress Cataloging-in-Publication Data

O'Kane, Trish
    Guatemala in focus: a guide to the people, politics and
    culture / Trish O'Kane
       p. cm. (In focus guides)
    Includes bibliographical references.
    ISBN: 1-56656-242-2 (paperback)
    1. Guatemala - Guidebooks. 2. Guatemala - Description and
    travel I. Title II. Series: In focus (London, England)
    F1463.6.035 1999
    917.28104'53--dc21   98-27653
                                               CIP

In the U.K.:

Latin America Bureau (Research and Action) Ltd,
1 Amwell Street, London EC1R 1UL

The Latin America Bureau is an independent research and publishing
organization. It works to broaden public understanding of issues of
human rights and social and economic justice in Latin America and the
Caribbean.

A CIP catalogue record for this book is available from the British
Library
ISBN: 1 899365 24 9

Editing: Marcela López-Levy
Cover photograph: Day of the Dead at Todos Santos, Paul Smith
Cover design: Andy Dark
Design: Liz Morrell
Cartography and diagrams: Kees Prins and Marius Rieff, and Catherine
Pyke

Already published in the *In Focus* series:
Argentina, Bolivia, Brazil, Chile, Colombia, Costa Rica, Cuba,
Dominican Republic, Eastern Caribbean, Ecuador, Jamaica, Mexico,
Peru, Venezuela

Printed and bound in Korea

CONTENTS

GLOSSARY

ASC	Civil Society Assembly
CACIF	Coordinating Committee of Agricultural, Commercial, Industrial, and Financial Associations.
CACM	Central American Common Market
CIA	US Central Intelligence Agency
CONAVIGUA	National Coordination of Guatemalan Widows
CONIC	National Indigenous and Campesino Coordination
CPR	Communities of the Population in Resistance
CUC	Committee for Campesino Unity
DCG	Guatemalan Christian Democrats
EGP	Guerrilla Army of the Poor
FAR	Armed Rebel Forces
FDNG	New Guatemalan Democratic Front
FRG	Guatemalan Republican Front
GAM	Mutual Support Group
MINUGUA	UN Human Rights Mission in Guatemala
ODHA	Archbishop's Human Rights Office
ORPA	Organization of the People in Arms
PAC	Civil Self-Defense Patrol
PAN	National Advancement Party
PSD	Socialist Democratic Party
REMHI	Truth Commission set up by Catholic Church
UCN	National Centrist Union
UFCO	United Fruit Company
URNG	Guatemalan National Revolutionary Unity

INTRODUCTION: THE NEW DAWN

"Let Us Rejoice" is the paradoxical title of a poem by Francisco Morales Santos, one of Guatemala's foremost contemporary poets. In it he enumerates the threats to life, dignity and freedom that have marked Guatemalan life. But he also powerfully celebrates the "right to dream" and the reasons why threats cannot quell life, ideals and relationships, "because nothing and no one can take the good away from us."

Guatemalan history reads like an unequal struggle between life and deathly silence. The European conquest brought disease, war and slavery to the indigenous population who revolted, resisted, and escaped ever further into the mountains and the forests. The geography of Guatemala still bears witness to those struggles, with the majority of the indigenous population living in remote, dispersed villages in the highlands while Ladinos occupy towns and cities. The highlands barely support a population of mainly subsistence farmers, but on the rich volcanic soils of the coastal plains, plantations extend as far as the eye can see. A history of division and domination has created a society rent by unequal access to resources, to land and to wealth. Only as recently as December 1996, peace was signed to end a 36-year-long civil war, marking the first step in the public non-violent acknowledgement of the polarization of Guatemalan society.

Outside the country, we know of the horrific human rights abuses on the one hand, and the romanticized, colorful indigenous culture used to attract tourists on the other, without sufficient in-depth explanation for either. The complexity of Guatemala, with its extremes and contradictions, is perhaps the reason why it fascinates outsiders. Not only the growing numbers of tourists who travel to see the beautiful indigenous woven cloth but not the person wearing the *traje*, but also the countless writers who have tried to make sense of the country's "terrible beauty." They have tried to make known the ongoing tragedy caused by poverty, discrimination and war, and the struggles to end them.

But over the last decade, Guatemalans have regained the political space in which to speak in their own voices. In particular, the sector of society that had been denied a place on the national stage, the indigenous majority, demanded their right to be heard. The peace process ending the civil war has created a framework for articulating calls for justice as well as peace, which may be the first step out of the violent cycles of repression that clouded earlier attempts to tackle inequality in Guatemala.

Maize crop and mange tout, Santa Apolonia, Chimaltenango   *Paul Smith/PANOS Pictures*

The indigenous movement has taken as its motif "a new dawn," the beginning of an epoch interpreted by their spiritual leaders from their ancient ritual calendar. The new dawn is a time for renewal and clarity, a time for re-establishing the history, culture and languages of the Maya. Moreover, it is a time for all Guatemalans to reassess how they are to live together on terms of equality and mutual respect. The legacy of authoritarianism and an economic system that places profits for a few before the development of the majority is not easy to overcome, but the new dawn promises the right to dream and new opportunities for change.

1 HISTORY: THE PEOPLE OF MAIZE

The Mayan population today is the largest American Indian group in Northern and Central America, totaling approximately six million. The word "Maya" refers to an historic family of languages as similar to each other as the Romance languages. The majority of the Maya, approximately five million, live in Guatemala. The term "Maya" has been adopted by the dynamic movement for ethnic rights in Guatemala, to counter the term *indio* used by others pejoratively. The rest of the descendants of the ancient Maya live in southern Mexico, Belize and western areas of El Salvador and Honduras.

Guatemalan history was first recorded for posterity in hieroglyphs on scrolls. They chronicled ancient myths and history before and after the Spanish conquest in 1524. The most complete Mayan creation text is the *Popol vuh* (*pop* is seat of authority, *vuh* means book). Known as the Bible of the Americas, it describes the genesis of the Mayan people as the outcome of four eras of creation and destruction. It was written in the sixteenth century and transcribed alphabetically from hieroglyphs into our alphabet by the Quiché elite. It mentions Christianity and Pedro de Alvarado's conquest, and aimed both at preserving Mayan culture and achieving concessions from the new ruling elite, the Spanish. The Quiché are just one of at least 21 different ethnic groups belonging to the Mayan family, and were the most powerful when the Spanish arrived.

The creation story has many levels, from the mythical description of the beginning of time, to the origins of the Quiché people and post-conquest history. The Quiché are part of the people of maize, and their creation myth celebrates the greatest agricultural achievement of American native peoples, the domestication of maize. In mist-covered highland villages, the first sound to be heard before dawn is still the local maize mill. Women line up in the dark to grind their maize, boiled with lime, into a dough called *nixtamal*, and then head home to prepare tortillas for breakfast.

Around 2000BC what archeologists call the Mayan Pre-Classic period began. The Maya were becoming adept at some of the arts that later made them famous, such as pyramid building and hieroglyphics. One of the Americas' greatest archeological sites dating from this period is Kaminaljuyu, a huge pre-classic Mayan city located close to the heart of what is now Guatemala City. Most of the several hundred ceremonial temple mounds have been eaten up by freeways, luxury hotels, shopping centers, slums, and hamburger joints, but an area has been protected by the government and is open to tourists. Despite the urban setting, Mayan priests today continue to use Kaminaljuyu for ceremonies. Indigenous activist Rigoberta Menchú celebrated her Nobel Peace prize in 1992 with a gathering in Kaminaljuyu.

The Classic Maya

The Classic Period followed from AD 250 through AD 900, when the Maya reached the pinnacle of their development and power. A wealthy elite class emerged, boosted by the growth in long-distance trade. Mayan cities were graced with stone palaces with vaulted ceilings, the walls covered in colorful murals. The ruins of Tikal, deep in the northern Petén jungle, bear witness to the extraordinary architectural achievements of the Maya.

The ancient Maya have fascinated archeologists and anthropologists because of many distinguishing cultural traits: hieroglyphic writing, extensive manuscripts made of fig-bark paper or deerskin, a complex calendar, accurate astronomical knowledge, extensive trade and specialized markets, human sacrifice by beheading or removal of the heart, self-mutilation by drawing blood from the ears, tongue, or penis, and a pantheistic religion. For the modern Maya, the knowledge of the richness of their culture before the Spanish invasion aids in the process of renewal of their culture in the late twentieth century.

One of the most enduring achievements of the Classic Period is the Mayan calendar, which is still in use today. Mayan shamans or "daylords" (keepers of the calendar) are still consulted after deaths and before marriages, and for advice on illnesses, business deals, and the selection of leaders, in order to ensure success by determining the right day for action.

The Maya have always been students of time. In order to measure time and its effect on their lives, they have a calendar with two cycles: one secular or solar, and another sacred. The solar cycle is a 365-day year, divided into eighteen months of twenty days each, with a highly feared five-day unlucky period at the end. The sacred cycle lasts 260 days, and a sequence of the numbers one through thirteen are matched with twenty named days. The combination of the number and the day has a particular meaning that affects the life of a person born that day and determines their personality and aptitudes.

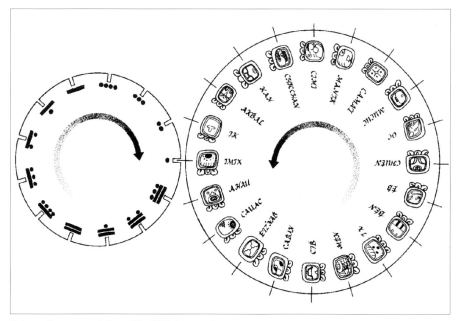

Schematic representation of the 260-day count

Courtesy Thames & Hudson

The Mayan Calendar

A young Mayan couple are nervous as they wait to hear the verdict of the wizened old man who is the daylord in their village. He sits at a low wooden table in his thatch-roofed hut, with his divining bag full of seeds and crystals in front of him. While reciting a prayer, he spreads the seeds and the crystals out, rolls and mixes them in a counterclockwise direction, and then makes piles. The couple hold their newborn son, whom they hope was born on a favorable day, and will live to overcome the hardships of hunger and war that they have lived through. If the date is not auspicious, they are prepared to do the necessary rituals to counteract the bad influences.

The verdict is complex. It is not just a matter of being born on a good or bad day. The daylord explains that their son was born on Ak'abal, the day of "dawn" or "opening," which also means "to blame" or "conceal." Their child will be feminine in character, wealthy, verbally skillful, and possibly a liar, cheat, or complainer. Since he was born on Ak'abal, he will have the special gift of "lightning," meaning he will be able to answer questions regarding the past or future through interpreting the jumping or twitching of his own muscles or bloodstream. This son, the daylord advises them, would make a good priest-shaman, road-guide, or marriage spokesman.

The Mysterious End of the Classic Maya

From the inscriptions left on ruins, it seems that the Mayan intelligentsia were at their peak when their great cities suddenly collapsed. In the ninth century, an unexplained set of events meant that within 100 years the great Mayan cities were abandoned. Archeologists can all only agree that the collapse happened. Theories abound about possible epidemics, Mexican invasions, social revolution and natural disasters.

Archeological discoveries, particularly in Petén, show that the population more than doubled during the period just prior to the crisis. The exhaustion of the soil due to intensive farming could have coincided with a labor shortage, as workers were forced to the cities to satisfy cultural and religious demands. Mayanists who believe that overpopulation and environmental degradation led to the Mayan apocalypse point to the ominous lessons for humanity today. The Mayan collapse was an example of a culture that abused its natural resources in an environment that requires care to be replenished. If the Maya did suffer from overpopulation, overexploit their environment, and destroy their own livelihoods, their plight bears great parallels to modern environmental concerns.

Following the cataclysm, the remaining Mayan settlements suffered a wave of invasions by Mexican Toltecs. Ancient documents of the Quiché describe how around AD 1225, Toltec warriors and priests entered the Guatemalan highlands. Allied to the invaders, the Quiché extended their empire and dominated other Maya groups. The Quiché kingdom was at its peak around AD 1450, just 70 years before the Spanish arrived in Guatemala.

Divided and Conquered

The Maya were briefly spared from the Spanish *conquistadores*, who initially flocked to Mexico in search of gold. The Spanish conquest of Guatemala began in 1524 with the arrival of Pedro de Alvarado, who was famed among his peers for his cruelty. The Spanish had a harder time defeating the Maya than the Aztecs, as the Mexican Aztecs had one central authority, and when their leader Moctezuma fell, the empire went with him. The Maya, however, were organized in small independent kingdoms, each with its own leader. They fought like jungle guerrillas, setting traps at night and ambushing the invaders.

When the Spanish arrived, the Quiché domain covered 16,000 square miles and controlled the lives of close to a million people. The Quiché tried to form a united front against the Spanish with some of the other Mayan groups, like the Kakchiqueles and Tzutuhiles, but were betrayed by the former. Contemporary Maya still mourn this tragedy and point to

A view of Tikal

the imperative need for unity. Even if the Quiché had managed to ally themselves with other ethnic groups, they probably could not have withstood the technical superiority of the Spaniards, who had horses and guns. During one long battle, de Alvarado personally killed the Quiché leader Tecún Uman, and the Quiché surrendered.

The Spaniards were helped by the fact that the Maya were already severely physically debilitated by the time of the conquest. European epidemics brought over from Europe, such as chickenpox, measles, typhoid, bubonic plague, and other maladies had spread to Guatemala from Mexico, and Mayan documents recount the deaths of thousands even before de Alvarado's arrival. It is estimated that the indigenous population of Central America was reduced from fourteen million at the arrival of the Spanish to two million in two generations.

Reign of Terror

Despite being greatly outnumbered by the Maya, the Spanish were able to impose the colonial system through a reign of terror. This was amply documented by Spanish priests sent to the Americas with the secret mission of reporting the real conditions to the Spanish crown, as the King did not trust the glowing reports of his *conquistadores* that the Maya were happy and flourishing. One such investigative crusader was Archbishop Cortés y Larraz, who in his secret report to King Carlos III on the treatment of the Maya wrote in 1770: "...they are whipped for anything that anyone does not like. Of the cruelty I cannot give any testimony other than the fact that frequently I hear their cries and weeping from my room, and the distant lash of the whip, and I cannot contain my emotions..."

Larraz added that when he first arrived in Guatemala, he was surprised by the fact that the Maya never answered "yes" or "no" to a question but always "who knows," "maybe," or "could be" and he concluded that: "They live in such fear that they do not answer with the truth, but according to the wishes of the person asking the question..." This observation still holds true in many parts of the Guatemalan countryside as a result of the modern-day army's more recent reign of terror.

The Colonial Period

Since Guatemala had few get-rich-quick resources such as gold and silver, the focus of the Spanish conquest was the forced labor of the Indian population. As taxation was the single most important source of income for the Spanish crown in Guatemala, the Spaniards' immediate concern following the conquest was to set up a system of domination which guaranteed slaves to work the land and pay taxes.

The Spanish extracted labor from the indigenous population through several institutions. The first was the *tributo*, a tax that had to be paid twice a year by all men 18 to 50 years old. Only Mayan nobles and mayors were exempted; in fact, Guatemala was the only Spanish colony where women also had to pay the tax. Payment was usually made in the form of goods such as beans, maize, chickens, blankets, and other articles. Another was the *repartimiento*, from the Spanish verb *repartir,* meaning to distribute. Under this system, land was distributed to the Spanish *conquistadores*, and a number of Mayans were "allocated" to those farms. Every Sunday after Mass, all Mayan men of working age had to gather outside the church to be "distributed" for the week to toil in mines and public works. Mayors and the sick were exempt. However, since the infirm had to pay a substitute, poor health was a luxury few could afford. A complementary institution was the *pueblo* (village) where the Maya were forced to live. Before the conquest, most Maya lived in scattered settlements. The Catholic Church organized the *pueblos* to ease the conversion of the pagan Maya to the one true Faith, but the *pueblos* also served to guarantee a captive labor force and tax-paying population.

The system was structured to exploit the indigenous population without destroying it. Strictly speaking, a man should have worked one week a month for the Spanish, with three weeks left to work his own land. How-

Woman wearing her *traje*, Santiago Atitlán   *Paul Smith*

ever, because work conditions were harsh, Spanish landowners cruel, and Mayan nobles apt to force poor Maya to replace them, the reality was very different. Mayan women were also forced to perform such tasks as threading raw cotton, prompting the Franciscans to complain to the Spanish crown that women worked day and night to meet deadlines, and the work distracted them from religious learning.

"Heading for the hills" became a defense mechanism for the Maya to escape enslavement, and thus dispersion became pronounced following conquest. The Spanish had to use their ingenuity to keep the Maya in the *pueblos* – and they found a way with the traditional *traje* or indigenous dress. As each area had particular symbols and colors embroidered in the cloth, they were easily identifiable and so the beautiful Guatemalan embroidered blouses were utilized to monitor people's movements. In the 1980s the Guatemalan army used similar techniques to control the indigenous population and force them to stay in "strategic hamlets."

The conquerors required unconditional Mayan acceptance of the authority of the Pope and the Spanish crown as rulers of the land, renouncing their own Gods and rulers. Non-compliance meant death, or at best, slavery. They were not content with a forced labor system and sought to legalize enslavement through a document known as the "Requirements of Palacios Rubios," named after the industrious Spanish lawyer who wrote it: "With the help of God we will enter powerfully against you, and we will make war on you everywhere and in every way, and we will make you, your women and children, slaves, and we will take your goods, and we will do all the harm to you that we can as vassals who do not obey or even accept God..."

In 1663 the Spanish King tried to abolish slavery in the colonies for fear that his over-zealous conquerors were going to wipe out indigenous people, and the crown would lose future tax-payers. The *criollo* (creole) class, those of Spanish descent born in Guatemala, fought fervently against the abolition of slavery, arguing that it was necessary to induce the native population to work. In their reports to the Spanish King, *criollos* said the Maya would spend all their time in drunken orgies if not forced to work. The *criollos* were terrified of the possibility of a free labor system in which salaries would have to be paid.

Although the names changed and the system altered slightly, forced labor was a reality in Guatemala well into the twentieth century. These colonial institutions have marked Guatemalan social structures deeply, creating two Guatemalas, separate and unequal.

Independence: Reforms for Whom?

Independence from Spain (1811-1821) is widely seen as having only benefited the local ruling class who no longer had to pay taxes to the crown. Meanwhile the indigenous population continued to be exploited by the landowning class of Spanish origin, the *criollos* (creoles) and the *mestizos* (of mixed blood), known in Guatemala as Ladinos, who had risen into the elite. Independence was triggered, as in the rest of Latin America, by Napoleon's invasion of Spain and subsequent political instability in the Iberian peninsula. The first declaration of independence was negotiated by the last of the rulers appointed by the Spanish, and upheld deeply conservative values, safeguarding the control of the Catholic Church in the country. In 1823, another independence act was brought in by liberals seeking reforms, as part of a Central American federation which rapidly fell apart.

In spite of constant struggles between Conservatives and Liberals, colonial structures remained virtually intact until the Liberal reform of 1871, when the first attempts were made to modernize the emerging state. Church lands were expropriated, a secular state was established with a public education system, and the civil, penal, commercial and fiscal codes were reformed. A national army was created, and basic infrastructure — a telegraph system, ports, and roads — planned.

One of the enduring legacies of the conquest was the immediate and forced appropriation of all land for the Spanish crown. Land could be acquired only through a royal concession, though the Spanish monarch set aside communal lands for indigenous Guatemalans, so they could produce their own food supply and sustain themselves in order to provide forced labor. Even these Indian lands, however, were progressively whittled away. In the nineteenth century, *criollos* and Ladinos acquired vast tracts of land to set up plantations to produce export crops. Legislation safeguarding indigenous communal lands was abolished, technically turning the rural population into an unemployed mass of migrant farm workers. At the same time, wealthy Ladinos moved onto Mayan lands and into towns, as they gained economic and political power locally and nationally.

Coffee Takes Over

Communal lands were further jeopardized in the 1870s, when the coffee boom changed land use patterns. President Justo Rufino Barrios imperiled communal lands in 1877, though most indigenous communities had no idea of the impact of the laws written in Spanish in the capital and continued working their lands as they had for centuries. They soon found themselves evicted by coffee growers, many of them German and Swiss, or Ladinos with good contacts in the government. Coffee became more disruptive for the indigenous communities than previous export crops, such as cochineal and indigo, which grew in the tropical lowlands. Coffee required higher altitudes, which meant that the mainly indigenous highlands became the target of plantation expansion. Coffee plantations also required many more workers, so a new workforce was created, made of landless peasants, or owners of lands too small for subsistence. By the end of the century, the little brown bean had become central to the economy, accounting for 80 percent of all exports. In 1997, coffee was still the most important export crop, accounting for a quarter of the income from exports.

Foreign control of the economy increased in the first decades of this century. The United Fruit Company (UFCO), a Boston-based banana company, negotiated a grant of extensive prime agricultural land in return for building the railroad it needed to ship out the cash crop. By the 1930s, UFCO was the largest employer, landowner, and exporter in Guatemala, and controlled the only railroad and Caribbean port. Technological development in general was not geared toward benefiting the majority, but rather toward continuing to ensure access to labor and underwrite foreign and elite economic interests. For example, the first telephones lines in Guatemala were installed so that coffee plantation owners could contact local authorities in highland towns to find Mayan workers.

Between 1931 and 1944, forced labor continued under the infamous dictatorship of Jorge Ubico, who believed he was a reincarnation of Napoleon. Ubico instituted a vagrancy law punishing landless Maya if they did not work 150 days per year on plantations. The Maya had to carry

Raking coffee beans to dry them   *Sean Sprague/PANOS Pictures*

a book in which the plantation owner noted the days worked or they were subject to arrest. In 1932 Ubico introduced Decree 1816, which exempted landowners from the consequences of any action taken to protect their goods or land, effectively legalizing the murder of rebellious Maya who resisted forced labor.

Resistance and Rebellion

The Maya developed a culture of resistance that ensured the survival of their own traditions within the Spanish colonial state. Since the conquest in 1524 there have been Indian rebellions on average every sixteen years. Within Guatemala, the Maya are depicted as a passive people who were easily conquered, and little has been written about the Mayan rebellions that have taken place continuously over the last five centuries. The image of passivity is a historical fallacy, appealing to the Ladinos who still hold power and fear a massive uprising by the Maya.

The Guatemalan struggle for independence from Spain fueled various indigenous rebellions by Maya who also wanted to benefit. A group of Momostecan rebels numbering nearly 600, including women leaders, established political alliances and participated in a rebellion in Totonicapán in 1820, during which Atanasio Azul was crowned king of the Quiché. In less remote areas, the Maya formed *pajuides,* temporary settlements hidden in mountainous valleys, and lived constantly on the move to avoid being forced into the *pueblos.* During the terrible repression of the 1980s, many Maya reverted to this practice to avoid army massacres, and for years mobile communities defended themselves by hiding in the jungle. Three out of four Maya today live in dispersed villages, and the urban centers organized by the Spanish were left to the Ladinos. Another historical form of resistance was suicide — conquerors in their chronicles to the crown told of Mayan men who preferred to kill their entire families, and then commit suicide, rather than submit to slavery.

Silence as Resistance

Ladinos still complain that the Maya are a distrustful, sullen, and silent race. Severo Martínez, a Guatemalan historian who wrote *La Patria del Criollo* (The Land of the Creole) about the colonial period, sees their silence as a form of resistance. Martínez uses this sad tale from the conquest to make his point.

The Mayan population of Motocintla, Huehuetenango, had always known of the existence of a nearby gold mine. But with the arrival of the Spanish, gold meant disaster. If the Spanish found out about the mine, an invasion of miners would descend on the town like a plague, force the Maya to mine it, and literally work them to death. The community vowed to guard the secret at all costs.

However, a Spanish priest sent to Motocintla slowly gained the confidence of the locals, and eventually convinced them to take him blindfolded to the mine. There he filled his pockets with gold nuggets, and gratefully swore never to divulge the secret to Spanish authorities. But he broke his promise and a flood of gold-seekers descended on the small town.

For eleven months the Spanish stayed in Motocintla, torturing and hanging local leaders to force them to take them to the gold mine. Their efforts were useless, and they later wrote complaining of the incredible stubbornness of the Maya. One by one, the leaders resisted with their silence, and died with their secret in order to save their families from enslavement.

Ten Years of Spring

It was not until 1944 that a Guatemalan government took account of the needs of the indigenous majority. Protests against the dictatorship of Ubico, begun by students but taken up by large sections of the population, brought in a democratic interlude which progressive Guatemalans still nostalgically recall as "the ten years of spring."

Ubico left a military junta in power and the protesters were joined by a group of young military officers to press for real democracy. The leader of the officers was Captain Jacobo Arbenz, who resigned from the army to protest its role in the military junta. Arbenz and his group distributed weapons to civilian volunteers, and on October 20, 1944, the President was forced to step down.

Juan José Arévalo, a charismatic university professor with more of a passion for literature than politics, did not offend upper-class sensibilities, which helped him win the elections held two months later. Arévalo gave flowery speeches about what he called "Spiritual Socialism," but never clearly defined his philosophy. He was anti-Communist, though he saw his country as an ally of the U.S. rather than a virtual colony. The reality was different. When Arévalo took power, U.S. companies owned and controlled the country's basic infrastructure: the railroad, its three most important ports, and the electricity company.

Between 1944 and 1954, Guatemala experienced its first taste of political pluralism. A multi-party system was established, trade unions were founded, and the majority of the population was able to vote for the first time. The two most important achievements of the Arévalo years were the Labor Code of May 1, 1947, which guaranteed the right to unionize, the right to strike, protection from unfair dismissal and a 48-hour week, and the creation of a social security system. The forced-labor system was abolished, and the Maya could now organize for a decent wage.

The changes provoked a virulent reaction from the highly conservative wealthy class, the Catholic Church, and the United Fruit Company (UFCO), whose interests were threatened by the new Labor Code. Banana workers began demanding better treatment and gained the right to strike. At that time United Fruit, which is better known as "the Octopus" in Central America, was the world's most important grower and exporter of bananas. The company's influence in the small Central American countries was tremendous and its annual budget was larger than that of any of the countries in which it operated. To protect its interests, UFCO became the leading voice in opposition to the dynamic nationalist leaders. Arévalo's Labor Code led the Octopus to cry communism, despite the fact that Arévalo himself was anti-communist. Although U.S. embassy officials in Guatemala at that time saw the Labor Code as fairly mild, McCarthyism was about to envelop Washington, and Guatemala would soon become the victim of Cold War hysteria.

Arévalo managed, however, to survive some 30 plots to overthrow him, thanks to the strong backing of the army, which was led by the young officer who had helped the civilian rebellion against Ubico, Jacobo Arbenz. Arbenz was backed as the next presidential candidate by several labor organizations and parties of the left. He had attracted their attention in 1947, when right-wing elements of the army wanted to expel labor leaders from the country and Arbenz effectively halted the purge. These organizations were impressed by his integrity, his defense of labor unions, and thought that with a progressive military officer in power even more radical changes could be made.

President Arbenz

That the Guatemalan army produced the most progressive, honest, and capable President in Guatemalan history to date is one of the country's great ironies. Arbenz was from a middle-class family which could not afford to send him to university, so he entered the military academy instead. CIA reports described him as brilliant and cultured. He had an open, probing mind and devoured books. He and his wife were both plagued by the knowledge that the social inequities in Guatemala needed to be changed.

U.S. officials had hoped that Arbenz would be an opportunist, and cultivate a close relationship with the U.S., as other Guatemalan officers had done in the past. But the CIA and the U.S. embassy had seriously misjudged his character. Before becoming President, Arbenz was close friends with several men who would later become the leaders of the Communist Party in Guatemala. Arbenz was attracted by the honesty, dedication, and principles of his Communist friends, as compared to the corruption of other political party leaders. Although he publicly declared on various occasions that he was not a Communist, the U.S. press, influenced by McCarthyism, quickly labelled him "Red Jacobo."

On March 15, 1951, Arbenz was inaugurated as President of Guatemala and announced that he would "transform Guatemala from a dependent nation with a semi-colonial economy into a country that is economically independent... from a backward country with a semi-feudal economy into a modern capitalist country, and proceed in a way which will ensure the greatest possible improvement in the standard of living for the great masses of our people."

Arbenz committed three great offenses in the eyes of the U.S. during his presidency. He carried out the first real agrarian reform in Central America and thereby affected the interests of the United Fruit Company. He had close personal ties with the Communist Party, although this party held no official positions of power in his government. And he insisted on

Arbenz making a public speech, early 1950s   AP

national sovereignty, and continually refused to support the U.S. in international forums. Guatemala would pay a terrible price for being one of the first countries in the hemisphere to act as a sovereign nation. Its experience was a warning to other Latin American nationalists who later attempted to defy the U.S.

On June 17, 1952, the Guatemalan Congress passed Decree 900 and the country embarked on agrarian reform. The reform only covered large expanses of uncultivated land and landowners affected by it were to be compensated by government bonds. The amount of compensation depended on the value of the land as it was declared for tax purposes. As landowners had consistently cheated on taxes by undervaluing their land, their compensation was meaningless. According to State Department documents, the reform affected a minority of landowners, only about 1,710 people. These few, however, owned over half of the private land in Guatemala.

By June 1954, when Arbenz was overthrown, 25 percent of the arable land in Guatemala had been expropriated. The reform had only affected the largest landowners, most of them absentee, and benefited approximately one sixth of the population with land and agricultural credits for production. As Arbenz expert Piero Gleijeses described it, the experience was unprecedented in Latin America, where significant land redistribution has been extremely rare and the provision of credit to poor peasants even rarer.

Despite predictions by Arbenz's enemies that the agrarian reform and public spending would negatively affect the economy, the opposite happened. Large landowners, fearing the confiscation of under-utilized lands, increased their production. The cultivation of subsistence crops increased substantially, and in 1953-54, Guatemala had the second greatest coffee crop in its history.

The CIA and Business as Usual

An alliance of the most conservative sectors in Guatemala, the Catholic Church, landowners, and much of the army, provided the local impetus for a CIA-engineered overthrow, known as Operation Success. Given that the Guatemalan civilian right-wing opposition to Arbenz was weak and disorganized, the CIA geared its plan toward the Guatemalan army, and encouraged it to betray Arbenz. Through press campaigns, rumor-mongering and other tactics, the CIA waged psychological war on Guatemalan army officers both loyal and opposed to Arbenz. Some officers, convinced that U.S. Marines would invade if Arbenz did not step down, betrayed their commander-in-chief. At the same time the U.S. imposed economic sanctions against Guatemala and pressured other Latin American countries to isolate the country internationally. The U.S. press depicted the nationalist Arbenz government as the first stronghold of Stalinism in the Americas.

On June 27, 1954 Arbenz resigned and took refuge in the Mexican embassy. A few months later he left the country with only his dignity intact. At the Guatemala City airport he was forced to strip to his underpants, and hand his clothes over, along with his military medals. His wife had to leave her personal jewelry. He drowned in his bath in mysterious circumstances in Mexico City in 1971.

In the days that followed Arbenz's resignation, different military leaders tried to take control. The U.S. embassy had the last word, choosing anti-Communist officer Colonel Carlos Castillo Armas. Armas immediately initiated an anti-Communist witch-hunt throughout the country. Thus began the more than three decades of terror that have kept Guatemala in the international headlines, with a toll of at least 100,000 dead, 40,000 disappeared, and hundred of thousands in exile.

In 1995, on the 51st anniversary of the October revolution, Arbenz's remains were finally brought back to rest in Guatemala. Thousands turned out to pay homage to the only President who tried to right colonial wrongs. People of all ages fought to carry the coffin, while others lined the streets and threw red carnations. Older Guatemalans cried as they remembered the suffering that the CIA coup caused them. "I was seven when the CIA overthrew Arbenz, and I remember my parents, who were very anti-Communist, cheering when he gave his farewell speech on the radio and left the country. How shortsighted they were, and how different our lives would have been if he had been permitted to carry out those reforms. How many lives has this cost us?" said one man bitterly.

2 POLITICS: IN THE SHADOW OF THE ARMY

The Long Night of Military Rule

The end of the political "Spring" (1944-54) meant not only the end of the first participatory experiment in democracy, but also the eradication of any vestige of reform in Guatemala. Tens of thousands of union organizers, political and indigenous activists, and other suspected left-wingers were immediately arrested, jailed, and many of them tortured and murdered. Political parties were dissolved overnight, and grassroots organizations were persecuted. Nearly all the land handed out to landless *campesinos* during Arbenz's agrarian reform was returned to its original owners. Zealous anti-Communists burned piles of "subversive" literature in the streets, while the U.S. embassy in Guatemala worked closely with the armed forces. The CIA operation was estimated to have cost between 80 and 90 million dollars.

The country plunged into a 30-year nightmare of military rule and severe repression of the left. Guatemala had become a showcase of U.S. policy in the Cold War fight against Communism. With the exception of the election of a civilian president in 1966, between 1954 and 1985 all heads of state were military men, and the political system was utterly dominated by the army. Political participation was severely restricted, electoral fraud was common, and the vast majority of the population did not vote. Parties on the left were banned, and even centrist parties such as the Christian Democrats suffered severe repression.

Armed Resistance

The exclusion of the majority from electoral politics meant dissatisfied Guatemalans could see no option other than to take up arms. Young nationalist army officers were critical of the corruption in the army hierarchy and their dissatisfaction grew into a revolt within the Guatemalan army on November 13, 1960. The uprising was led by two young lieutenants, 22-year-old Marco Antonio Yon Sosa and 19-year-old Luis Turcios Lima, both of whom later founded Guatemala's guerrilla movement.

The revolt lasted four days and was put down with U.S. help. Ironically, the revolt's leaders, Yon Sosa and Turcios Lima, were both trained by the U.S. army shortly before launching the uprising. They continued to organize clandestinely, forming the first guerrilla movement. They believed they could easily take over military installations, quickly overthrow the government, and force a return to democracy. They had no idea that they were about to begin one of the longest civil wars in the Western Hemisphere.

The rebels did not have the firepower, numbers or organizational structure to confront the Guatemalan army and were forced to retreat into the countryside. Students and *campesinos* began joining the movement en masse in 1962, and the widespread protests were met with severe repression. In late 1962, the guerrillas joined forces with an armed group of students and the communist Guatemalan Workers Party. The alliance was called the Armed Rebel Forces (FAR), one of the four guerrilla factions which signed the peace accords in 1996. The FAR's program was not openly socialist, but an extension of the Arbenz reforms. FAR leaders called for a national democratic revolution, with economic development based on industrialization and capitalism.

The guerrillas were racked by internal conflicts and divisions, which last to this day. Most of the differences were between those who believed in the viability of the electoral system, and those who were becoming increasingly radicalized by their first-hand experience of rural poverty. By 1964 some of the leadership openly espoused socialism.

In the late 1960s, the Guatemalan army, with heavy U.S. support, carried out a major offensive to wipe out the insurgents. U.S. military advisors provided technology imported from the Vietnam War, and napalm was used on the highland forests to destroy the guerrilla's cover. Washington did not want another nationalist revolution like Cuba's in its backyard. The offensive was largely successful in disabling the guerrillas.

In the 1970s the guerrillas began to build up a social base among the indigenous population, all the while explaining the reasons for their struggle. Two new guerrilla organizations were formed in 1972, the Guerrilla Army of the Poor (EGP) in Ixcán, and the Revolutionary Organization of the People in Arms (ORPA), in Sololá and San Marcos. By 1981, military intelligence sources believed that the guerrillas had the support of some 260,000 people in 35 counties in the northwestern highlands. In rural areas the guerrillas were burning municipal buildings as a challenge to the state's local power structures, while in Guatemala City urban units carried out sabotage operations. With a successful revolution in Nicaragua in 1979, and a major guerrilla offensive underway in neighboring El Salvador, many believed that 1981 would also be the year of revolution in Guatemala. They had gravely underestimated how the Guatemalan army would react.

The Guatemalan Army: Made in the USA

Before the 1944 revolution, the Guatemalan Army was a ragtag crew of some 6,000 forcibly drafted Mayan soldiers. At the height of the war in the 1980s, it had swelled to 51,600 men, including 3,000 military police and a network of approximately one million civilians in armed Civil

Defense Patrols. All Guatemalan men aged from 18 to 60 had to serve regularly in the patrols, which were the main mechanism for spying on and controlling the population. With these patrols, the army became a pervasive presence in every targeted community, through informers known as *orejas* (ears), who reported regularly to the local military base.

During the Arévalo-Arbenz period the army became more professional, and officers prided themselves on being part of "the army of the revolution." Arbenz, a military man himself, treated the army well. But the threats of the U.S. embassy to invade Guatemala weighed more heavily than scholarships abroad and discount stores for military personnel. The army opted to serve elite interests rather than Arbenz, and was rewarded with U.S. aid and training.

In the 1960s, in response to the growing guerrilla movement, the U.S. helped to modernize the Guatemalan army, providing helicopters, jeeps, radar, and other military hardware, as well as advice and training. The role of the U.S. in the post-coup years was significant and crucial in communications and intelligence. U.S. military trained the Guatemalan army in counter-insurgency tactics. They also helped to establish the intelligence practices that were to become a terrifying part of the state's repressive apparatus.

The U.S. military used Guatemala as a showcase of their counter-insurgency policy during the 1960s and 1970s and again during the Reagan era. It was in the period between 1966 and 1974 that the largest number of U.S. military personnel were present in Guatemala and the most assistance given. U.S. support continued until the late 1970s, when an emphasis on human rights surfaced in Washington's foreign policy and U.S. military aid was abruptly cut off to Guatemala. U.S. allies such as Israel and Taiwan quickly filled the vacuum, however, providing weapons and training to the Guatemalan army throughout the 1980s.

The U.S. financed civic action programs that distributed food and medicines, and also encouraged the army to do public works such as building roads, schools, and bridges. These programs set an important precedent for the Guatemalan army to move into civilian spheres — one that continues to be used in the 1990s as an argument to justify the need for a large peacetime army. As defense ministers scramble to protect their large budgets, soldiers are presented to the public as potential tree planters, garbage collectors, and tow-truck operators.

In the late 1960s, several anti-Communist death squads appeared, such as the feared "White Hand." Military officers were widely believed to be the driving force behind the death squads, although the economic elite supported these groups financially. Moreover, the army also openly carried out killings such as the 1966 murder of 28 intellectuals and union leaders who were thrown into the ocean from Air Force planes.

In the 1970s the army established firm control over state institutions. The Presidential High Command, an elite military guard set up on the premise of protecting the president, was actually a mechanism used throughout the 1980s and 1990s to control civilian presidents, who became virtual hostages of this corp. Another feared institution was the "archive," which was located in a building off Guatemala City's main square. The archive was run by military intelligence (G-2), and many Guatemalans believe that if they ever participated in politics, went to a protest, or exhibited otherwise "subversive" behavior, it was recorded there. In the mid-1990s, the government announced that it was dismantling the archive, but the institution has left a legacy of fear and created a culture of self-censorship.

The 1980s: the Guatemalan Holocaust

Despite U.S. military aid and massive repression, the guerrilla was still a threat in 1980. The Guatemalan army could not defeat the insurgents on the battlefield, or destroy their support networks. By the end of the 1970s, the rebels had recovered from the repression of the 1960s, and extended their social base into new areas of the country. The army decided to try new tactics.

On January 31, 1980, a group of peasant organizers peacefully occupied the Spanish embassy in Guatemala City to draw international attention to the fierce repression in the countryside. The embassy was surrounded by security forces and a fire mysteriously started. The Spanish ambassador barely escaped and all the protestors either died in the fire or were shot. Nobel Peace Prize winner Rigoberta Menchú was a young domestic worker in the capital at the time. Her father, one of the peasant leaders, died along with 38 others. One peasant survived only because he was buried under the charred corpses, and was taken to the hospital to be treated for his burns. The same night he was dragged out by armed men and his mutilated body was dumped the next day at the national university.

Guatemala became an international pariah. At the time, the country was run by General Fernando Romeo Lucas García, who was widely considered by Guatemalans to be the most bloodthirsty of the series of generals who had run the country since 1954. In the cities, Chevrolet vans with dark windows prowled the streets and the term "to be disappeared" became starkly current. Body dumps cropped up around the country. The morgues were filled to overflowing.

In the countryside, the army was preparing to carry out a "scorched earth policy," to eliminate the social support for the guerrillas. A series of massacres were carried out by the army and the civilian patrols throughout

Guerrillas of the URNG

1981 and 1982. In 1982 the four active guerrilla factions joined forces to create the Guatemalan National Revolutionary Unity (URNG), but it was too late. The URNG's social base had been destroyed, and the military defeat of the guerrillas was even more devastating than in the 1960s, and final. From then on, the URNG became a political force rather than a military threat.

The scorched earth counter-insurgency campaign that began under Lucas García continued with General Ríos Montt. Guatemalans called it *la escoba* (the broom), because the army swept the country in a wave of terror, burning hundreds of villages, massacring thousands, driving hundreds of thousands of refugees across the Mexican border, and creating many more internally displaced. *La escoba* became a holocaust. Human rights organizations estimate that at least 30,000, mostly Mayan, Guatemalans were murdered by the army in the 1980s. In addition to the refugees in Mexico, many fled to the capital and hid in slum areas. Others took to the jungle, forming mobile communities known as Communities of Population in Resistance, to escape army bombings and repression.

With the guerrilla threat under control, by 1982 some military officers became convinced that it was too costly for the army to exert power directly. It seemed generals-turned-presidents soon forgot the army's institutional needs, and became ambitious and corrupt politicians rather than soldiers. The military exercise of power was also very damaging in terms of international public relations. Moreover, the country was going into

Soldiers hand out guns to civilian patrol members, 1987 *Joe Fish*

economic decline, and investment and aid were required. A long-term strategy for the army to withdraw from direct participation in government was planned, in order to permit some form of democracy. The strategy contemplated an eventual transition to civilian rule controlled by the army.

The international press paid more attention to Ríos Montt and the bloodshed of the period 1982-83 than to Lucas García's reign of terror from 1978-1982. This was probably because Ríos Montt was a much more colorful personality than Lucas García, and provided good quotes. Ríos Montt became a fundamentalist Christian during the 1970s when he joined the sect *El Verbo*, which was linked to the U.S.-based Gospel Outreach, and he later became the first Protestant president of Guatemala. He brought state violence into the public arena by putting "subversives" before firing squads. While many Guatemalans grimace at the mention of Ríos Montt's name, others praise him fervently as an Evangelical law-and-order savior, which goes some way to explaining his political party's massive following in the last two elections.

In the early 1980s, the officers who supported Ríos Montt hoped he would pave the way for a transition to a civilian president. Ríos Montt had been known as a reformer in the army in the 1970s, and admired for his dynamism and oratory skills. But once in power, he showed no signs of following through with the plan, and provided an untenably high profile for the role of the army in human rights violations. Worse still, he alienated powerful sectors by introducing taxes. In spite of having provided key military successes in the counter-insurgency war, on August 8, 1983, eighteen months after taking power, Ríos Montt was overthrown and replaced by General Mejía Victores. The Ríos Montt experience confirmed that a move towards a controlled democracy was the option backed by the most powerful interests in the country, including sectors of the army.

But while the groundwork was being laid for an eventual return to a semblance of democracy, the army had already assured its long-term control over the rural population. It was during the Ríos Montt period that the vast network of Civil Defense Patrols was most active. The civil patrols took part in the army's rural development programs which forced thousands of displaced *campesinos* into "model villages." The Civil Defense Patrols, as the army's most devastating instruments of control, were responsible for many of the human rights violations in rural areas. The patrols imposed new structures of authority in each village, usurping and undermining the clout of local mayors, Mayan priests, and other traditionally recognized leaders. They utterly changed the nature of rural society.

Prisoners in the Palace

In July 1984, as part of the transition to democracy, a special temporary Congress was elected for the purpose of writing a new constitution and electoral laws. General elections were held to elect a President and members of Congress in 1985, and Christian Democrat Vinicio Cerezo became Guatemala's first civilian president in two decades. From the beginning of his term in office Cerezo attempted to dispel any great expectations as to what he might be able to achieve. But even within the constraints placed by the army on the transition to democracy, his policies were lackluster. Observers noted that his main concern seemed to be how to remain in power, which involved attempting to keep the army, the business community and international observers happy, an impossible juggling act.

The change in 1986 to a civilian government did open the doors for cautious grassroots organizing and political participation. However, the legacy of three decades of repression, militarism and an authoritarian culture are not easily overcome, and in the 1990s, democracy was still weak in Guatemala. Most parties are electoral creatures that hibernate between elections, and appear a few months before the vote in rural areas when their paid activists hand out calendars, t-shirts and baseball caps with the image of their political *caudillo* (big man) emblazoned on them.

President Cerezo with the army high command   *Joe Fish*

The next President, Jorge Serrano, was an Evangelical follower of General Ríos Montt and his term reinforced the perceptions of the weaknesses of the new political system. On May 25, 1993, Guatemalans woke up to find that all radio stations were playing the same cryptic *marimba* music. The media had been taken over by the state, newspaper offices were surrounded by soldiers, tanks were cruising downtown streets, and the Congress had been dissolved by Serrano. Serrano attempted an "auto-coup" to hold on to power when faced with serious corruption charges. The move also coincided with pressure from hard-line military officers who hoped a coup would derail the peace talks between the government and guerrilla.

The Serrano coup was resolved in a whirlwind ten days of intrigue, during which the international community and the Guatemalan private sector pushed for a return to formal democracy. Serrano fled the country and a former human rights ombudsman, Ramiro de León Carpio, was elected as interim president by a special emergency Congress until the general elections in 1995.

De León's good image abroad as a human rights activist improved Guatemala's public relations overnight. But given the circumstances under which De León came to power, with no planning, political party or advisors to support him, he quickly became dependent on the military. Pretensions to limit the army's power were soon forgotten. One month after his inauguration, on July 3, 1993, De León's cousin, prominent politician Jorge Carpio, was murdered by a group of masked men. A civil patrol linked to the local army base was later found guilty of the crime. The message to the new president was clear: any attempts at real change could cost him his life or that of a family member. As UN human rights expert Christian Tomuschat commented during a visit to Guatemala in 1994, President De León was "a prisoner in the palace."

The Human Rights Challenge

The civilian facade promoted by the army after 1983 improved Guatemala's image, underwriting an inflow of international aid and foreign investment. The army could not control, however, the degree to which the civilian population took advantage of the new situation and began to push for real democracy. After the 1985 election, some Guatemalans in exile began returning to the country, and slowly the social network of grassroots organizations which had been wiped out in the early 1980s began to resurface.

In 1984, the Mutual Support Group (GAM) was founded, to organize the family members of the thousands of disappeared. Myriad other human rights organizations soon followed, led by the families of victims of the violence. One of the most important organizations to emerge, which continues to play a leading role in the late 1990s, is the National Commission of Guatemalan Widows (CONAVIGUA), an organization of Mayan women with a large support network in the countryside. CONAVIGUA has bused in thousands of Mayan women to the capital to protest against the military draft, forced patrolling, and army and paramilitary repression. The marches of determined women with babies on their backs in their *trajes* in front of the Congress and National Palace have become a mainstay of Guatemalan political life.

The human rights movement of the late 1980s pushed for real political participation in Guatemala. The movement also forged a new generation of political leaders to replace the generation lost to the repression of the late 1970s and 1980s. The organizations are well-connected with

Demonstration by the Mutual Support Group (GAM) in Guatemala City, mid 80s   *Joe Fish*

international human rights groups, and many of the leaders have suffered repression personally in their struggle to change the culture of terror.

Resurgence of Terror

A reaction from the right to grassroots activism was not long in coming. While part of the army's long-term strategy was to encourage civilian participation in political life, the assertiveness of the emerging organizations, and the politics of returning exiles, began to make army officers and conservative private sector leaders nervous. Democracy could not be as easily administered in small doses as they had planned, and the resurgence of critical thought and opinion in the country became threatening.

In 1989 and 1990, just a few years after the return to civilian government, the country slid back into bloodshed. In September 1989 nearly 30 university student leaders were disappeared. In 1990 some of the most notorious human rights violations occurred, turning into cases which still cause the Guatemalan army and government headaches today. This was the year Guatemalan anthropologist Myrna Mack was stabbed over 50 times by a member of the Presidential High Command.

Mack's murder had widespread repercussions in Guatemala and abroad, and was an ominous message to the emerging civil society. An academic from a wealthy Ladino family, Mack was one of the first researchers in Guatemala to carry out fieldwork in war zones. She pioneered reports on the impact of the war on displaced populations and refugees, testifying to the continuing repression in the communities despite the army's public relations campaign to the contrary. Mack also worked closely with the Catholic Church, which provided important support to the fledgling human rights organizations and the communities themselves.

The year 1990 ended with yet another act of horror, and also, of hope. The army killed thirteen Tzutuhiles in Santiago Atitlán and caused an international outcry. The community, with the backing of human rights organizations, demanded the army's withdrawal from the area. The local base was forced to shut down, and the hated civil patrol was disbanded. The Tzutuhiles organized their own local defense system known as the *ronda* (round) which served to sound the alarm whenever the army tried to violate a presidential order to stay out of Atitlán. Santiago became the first army-free town in the country, and set an important precedent for demilitarization.

Communities of the Population in Resistance

Myrna Mack's greatest affront to the army was to bring to public attention the plight of the Communities of the Population in Resistance (CPRs). The CPRs were the mobile communities that formed as a result of the massacres of the early 1980s, similar to the *pajuides* created by the Maya centuries earlier to escape the Spanish conquest. Thousands of *campesinos* fled army massacres and hid in the jungle, moving constantly to avoid army incursions and bombardments. As the war dragged on, rather than return to their homes and be forced to live in the "model villages" the army was forcing up to 50,000 people to move to, they formed communities with mobile schools, health clinics, and kitchens that could be dismantled at the slightest warning of the army's approach. Their crops were often burned by soldiers, and the CPRs lived in very difficult conditions for over a decade. In the early 1990s, the CPR leaders "came out into the clearings," as they describe it, and asked to be recognized as a non-combatant civilian population. By 1996, some of the CPRs had left their jungle homes and integrated into other rural communities.

The Fight for Justice – the Myrna Mack Case

The Mack case is a perfect example of how some Guatemalans have turned personal tragedy into a struggle to change their country. Following her sister's murder, Helen Mack has led a six-year legal struggle to put the generals who planned and ordered the killing in jail.

Jungle classroom: children in a CPR school   *Paul Smith*

In February 1993, Mack had her first victory. Noel Jesus Beteta, a 27-year-old army specialist, was sentenced to 30 years in prison for the Mack murder. The sentence came after an agonizing trial presided over by thirteen different judges in a period of over two years, most of whom resigned over threats, or asked for a transfer rather than make a ruling. Six witnesses went into exile, over 30 journalists received death threats, and the principal police investigator was shot dead in front of his headquarters days after signing the report incriminating Beteta. Despite it all, due to Helen Mack's perseverance, Beteta became the first member of the armed forces to be convicted for a political murder.

Although her chances of putting those who actually planned and ordered the crime behind bars are slim, Mack's struggle for justice has inspired many Guatemalans, and led to a wide recognition of the need to reform the Guatemalan justice system.

Rebuilding in the 1990s

Compared to the 1980s, the 1990s have been a decade of positive change, with the slow rebuilding of social networks and structures. The victims of army violence and their relatives have become an important social force, and are revitalizing Guatemalan civil society and electoral politics. They work alongside new organizations of Mayan activists, professional associations, women's groups, and *campesino* organizations. On a national level, these forces had a major impact on the 1995 general elections. For the first time since the Arbenz overthrow, the Guatemalan left was able to participate through the creation of a new political party, the Guatemalan National Democratic Front (FDNG), which came in third place for the presidency, won six seats in Congress, and mayoralties across the country. At the local level, "civic committees" were formed, local non-party groups which ran independent candidates for county seats.

These progressive forces within civil society were strengthened through their indirect participation in the peace negotiations between the government and the URNG. Although they were not present at the negotiating table, eleven social sectors were invited to join the Civil Society Assembly (ASC) in 1994: political parties, business associations represented by the Coordinating Committee of Agricultural, Commercial, Industrial, and Financial Associations (CACIF), religious groups, unions and popular organizations, academics and professionals, Mayan organizations, women's organizations, journalists, development NGOs, research centers, and human rights groups. Only the business sector refused to participate. The ASC was created as a consultative body to make recommendations to the two parties negotiating peace, and to provide civil society with a voice. In an unprecedented experiment in participatory democracy, the ASC spent thousands of hours debating issues related to the peace process, trying to build consensus. The process was fraught with difficulties but signaled the emergence of a more democratic political culture.

Returned Refugees

The returning refugees have become one of the most vocal new forces in civil society, much to the chagrin of the army and some large landowners. Over 100,000 Guatemalans crossed the Mexican border in the early 1980s, fleeing army violence. Many dispersed in Mexico, integrating themselves into Mexican communities. Many went farther north, swelling the ranks of Central American refugees in Los Angeles, Houston, and Chicago. Some 45,000 were recognized as refugees by the United Nations, and lived in camps in Mexico until the mid-1990s. In the 1990s, some decided to return home.

"We struggled to return, now we return to struggle," the first large group of 2,500 refugees chanted as they crossed the Mexican-Guatemalan border on January 20, 1993, with fists raised and music blaring from portable speakers. The 100 buses were filled with Mayans who had fled the massacres of the 1980s, and were now returning to their jungle homes in the Ixcán to rebuild their communities. The caravan crossed the country during a two-week journey which became the largest and most prolonged

Onlookers greet the returning refugees
Gail Deutsch/Sean Sprague Photography

political demonstration since the late 1970s, with thousands of Guatemalans lining the highway to greet the refugees with tears, banners, and gifts of food and clothing.

The organized return of refugees as communities, rather than as individuals or families, was important politically because it meant negotiating communal rights, free from military control. Before returning, the refugees had negotiated an agreement with the government guaranteeing them land, exemption from military service for three years, and exemption from civil patrolling. The return incorporated international accompaniment, with foreigners living in the returned communities as human rights observers. The returnees began to press for their rights in extremely isolated areas of the country, to protest the presence of military bases, and to pressure for their withdrawal. The communities effectively managed to create military-free zones.

Many had fled the country as extremely poor Mayan peasants, who did not speak or read Spanish. A decade later, they returned with a higher educational level than many other Guatemalans and as an organized political force with international backing. They settled in extremely isolated rural areas, and brought their own teachers, health promoters, and community leaders, who had all trained in Mexico. In some war zones the returnees exacerbated tensions instigated by army campaigns linking the refugees to the guerrilla movement. Often the extremely poor local population also resented the returnees because of their access to NGO development funding. But their level of political consciousness and social organization has had an impact on surrounding villages. In parts of the country where the repression had destroyed social organization, the returnees have organized local human rights committees, road-building committees, and encouraged villages to band together to push the government into complying with promises of rural development. They were, as many conservative Guatemalans had feared, "a bad example."

Despite the international accompaniment and the presence of a UN human rights mission throughout the country, the returnees' security could not be assured. On October 8, 1995, while the returned community of Xamán was celebrating its first anniversary, a patrol of 25 soldiers entered the village and shot and killed thirteen returnees, one of them an eight-year-old boy.

Digging Up the Truth

Horrible events such as this have probably served to strengthen the struggle that has been waged throughout the 1990s to know the truth about the Guatemalan holocaust. The state, and particularly the army, have tried to encourage a form of collective amnesia, "a cleaning of the slate," arguing that peace is not possible without burying the past. But the victims and their family members demand the right to know and to remember, and early in the decade, human rights groups began a series of efforts to dig up the truth.

A national anthropological forensic team was founded. The team began digging up clandestine mass graves across the country and publishing their findings. The Catholic Church also set up its own truth commission, called REMHI, which began working in 1995. Across the country, local church workers interviewed thousands of witnesses and victims, in an attempt to systematically document the massacres. The Church's investigation is designed to assist the official truth commission that was created through the peace process. Yet the most significant aim of the report of the project to rescue the historical memory of the communities most affected by violence is to help those communities mourn, be heard and move forward. The final report was presented in April 1998; entitled *Never Again*, it records 6,500 testimonies which describe more than 55,000 victims of the war. Over 90 percent of the victims were civilian leaders, and 75 percent of them were indigenous. Almost 80 percent of the victims recorded were killed between 1980 and 1983, and the greatest part of the violence was carried out by the army and the paramilitary structures they set up.

Two days after the presentation of the REMHI report, Monseñor Juan José Gerardi, the assistant bishop in charge of the project, was brutally murdered. In the aftermath of the worst political killing ever perpetrated

A Mayan priest blesses the mass grave of 200 victims, Rabinal, Baja Verapaz

Paul Smith/ PANOS Pictures

against the Church, Guatemala seemed poised at the edge of an abyss of violence and impunity. But the response to his murder was overwhelming. Thousands marched to his funeral, and human rights organizations formed a "Never Again" coalition to strengthen the call for an investigation, the end of impunity, and respect for human rights. Monseñor Gerardi became the most visible martyr of the struggle for justice.

Most Guatemalans do not expect to ever see those responsible for the holocaust behind bars. But they hope that at least if the names and details are published, it will serve as a moral deterrent to possible future human rights violators and initiate the crucial process of demilitarization.

The Peace Process

In the late 1980s, President Oscar Arias of Costa Rica promoted a regional peace proposal to end all the wars in Central America via negotiation. The Esquipulas peace process which Arias initiated was supported by the then Guatemalan President Vinicio Cerezo. Meanwhile the URNG was in retreat from the devastating impact of the army massacres and repression of the early 1980s. They were working outside Guatemala to establish themselves diplomatically as a political force, while drawing international attention to the human rights situation inside the country.

As a result of the Esquipulas agreements, in 1987, a National Reconciliation Commission was set up in Guatemala, and Cerezo agreed to talk directly with the URNG. It was the beginning of a long-winded and difficult peace process. The first seven years of talks yielded little in terms of concrete agreements, and the process was threatened several times by the still powerful army. However, the negotiations led to a political thawing in the country, and for the first time in decades various civic groups began to engage in public dialogue. In 1989 the Commission established a National Dialogue, providing a space for civil society to discuss the civil war and the peace negotiations. The Catholic Church became actively involved in promoting the peace process, lending it greater legitimacy. One of the founding members of the Commission was Bishop Quezada Toruño, representing the Guatemalan's Bishops' Conference, who went on to become the national mediator for the peace process.

The negotiations limped along without real advances until 1994, when the government of President Ramiro de Leon Cárpio and the URNG leadership invited the United Nations to moderate negotiations and verify all final agreements. The UN's involvement gave new life to the process, and over the next three years eight major accords, and a series of minor agreements were signed, committing the Guatemalan government to an agenda for the building of a more democratic and just state. In return, the guerrillas of the URNG agreed to turn in their arms and rejoin civilian society.

In March 1994 the first and most far-reaching accord was signed, committing the two parties (government and URNG) to respect human rights and permit the immediate presence of a UN human rights verification mission. By late 1994, the mission, called MINUGUA, had deployed over 200 international observers throughout the country, and opened thirteen offices, some in extremely isolated regions. Many observers were placed in areas where virtually the only state presence was the local army base, and soldiers and local authorities were used to bullying the population. The UN presence was an immediate deterrent and countered the army's impunity in rural areas. During the first three years of the mission, the number of human rights violations dropped dramatically.

The signing of the accord on indigenous rights also had an almost immediate impact due to the political significance of the growing Mayan movement (see Chapter 4). The agreement stated that the Maya have been "submitted to discrimination, exploitation and injustice," and have been denied political participation. The government agreed to launch a campaign to change "mind-sets and behavior," and to criminalize ethnic discrimination. A major gain was the state's recognition of indigenous languages and the promise to reform the education, justice, and other state services to better meet the needs of the Maya.

A day to march - the signing of the Peace Accords, 1996

Lin Knapp/Sean Sprague Photography

Two other extremely important accords were agreed, which if fully implemented, could significantly improve the quality of life of many Guatemalans. The first is the socio-economic accord, in which the government agreed to increase tax collection by 50 percent, and concurrently increase health and education budgets by the same amount. The second is "The Agreement on the Strengthening of Civilian Power and the Role of the Armed Forces in a Democratic Society," a very full title which covers many of the historical weaknesses of the Guatemalan state. The army must reduce its budget and personnel, as well as its presence in civilian tasks such as policing. The government agreed to create a new civilian police force and also to disarm and dismantle the Civil Defense Patrols.

In 1996, the army claimed to have 46,000 men in its ranks, although these numbers were widely considered to be exaggerated. The army's strategy seemed to be to overstate its numbers in order to avoid cutbacks. In 1997, the first "year of peace," common crime increased in Guatemala, and the army continued to play a highly public role in fighting it.

The Civil Defense Patrols were also disarmed and dismantled during 1996 by the army. The extent to which these networks were truly disarticulated remains a bone of contention, as the UN could not properly verify the process. It can be said that formally these patrols no longer exist, but in many villages it is probable that patrol leaders will continue to exert *de facto* power for quite some time.

On December 29, 1996 the final agreement on a "Firm and Lasting Peace" was signed, nearly ten years after the peace process was tentatively initiated. The final accord agreed constitutional and electoral reforms, the disarming and demobilization of the URNG and the ex-combatants' reinsertion into civil society. A timetable was also set for work on all the accords signed, giving the Guatemalan government until the year 2000 for full implementation.

Elections and Political Parties

In 1985 with the electoral mobilization of the army-controlled Civil Defense Patrols, turnout for elections was 48 percent, an all-time high in Guatemala. However, the 1990s average turnout has been 29.6 percent, the lowest in Latin America. Of the more than 20 political parties which stood in the November 1995 elections, these were the most significant:

• National Advancement Party (PAN) presents itself as the technocratic modernizing right, but includes protectionist business interests. Predominantly urban and Ladino, they have 43 seats in Congress.

• Guatemalan Republican Front (FRG) is the political vehicle for ex-president General Ríos Montt, who is presently barred from standing for President. FRG's populist, law-and-order rhetoric has attracted a considerable rural base. They lost only narrowly to the PAN's Alvaro Arzú in 1996. They have 21 seats in Congress.

• Guatemalan Christian Democrats (DCG) was discredited by charges of corruption following its transition-to-democracy government in 1986. DCG has since been in decline. DCG ran in coalition with the center-right Union del Centro Nacional (UCN) and Partido Socialista Democratico (PSD). Together this coalition has nine seats in Congress.

• New Guatemalan Democratic Front (FDNG) was the only left party to compete in the elections. Established just six months before the elections, it won six (of 80) congressional seats. It was formed by individuals and groups including intellectuals, professionals, URNG dissidents, and popular movement organisations. With popular movement leaders occupying the principal positions in the new party, the FDNG obtained significant support. It is the only left party in Congress.

Since the final peace accord was signed in December 1996, the URNG has demobilized and dissolved its constituent groups. In 1997 it began the process of becoming a political party. It is reticent about ideology and has dropped the socialist label, preferring to present itself as the democratic, multi-class expression of a new project of national unity, in which the main task is to ensure full compliance with the peace accords. The URNG's participation in the 1999 elections will represent a new departure in Guatemalan politics.

3   ECONOMY AND SOCIETY:
FROM BANANA TO BROCCOLI REPUBLIC

Guatemala's economy is the largest in Central America, but its social indicators tell a tragic story. Macroeconomic indicators for the country are good and continue to improve. The economy is growing, foreign investment is increasing, exports are successful and aid has been forthcoming from all major donors since the signing of the Peace Accords. The international community pledged almost two billion dollars between 1997 and the new millennium to underwrite the implementation of the accords, although to date the actual sum coming into Guatemala has been lower than expected. But Guatemala also has a marked inequality in the distribution of wealth.

Guatemala suffers from an extreme form of the regional legacy of the "banana republic": the vastly inequitable distribution of land and wealth, the uneven development, and the dependence on a few export crops and foreign investment. Guatemala has an economy beholden to the whims of the international market. For example, Guatemala is the world's largest cardamom producer, and when demand falters, small producers in jungle areas tighten their belts because they used their land to grow the "green gold" rather than maize for their own consumption. But Guatemala's social problems cannot only be laid at the door of international economic trends. The open economy is kept firmly in place by a national economic elite who rank amongst the most conservative and racist on the continent.

Guatemalan economic development continues to be based on a colonial model in which the economic elite extracts what it can from the land and underpaid workforce with little reinvestment in human or productive potential. Agricultural exports have fueled economic growth, particularly coffee, bananas, and cotton. By the 1980s agro-exports had been diversified to include cardamom, beef, sugar, and a variety of fruits and vegetables. In the 1990s, agricultural exports still accounted for a quarter of the Gross Domestic Product (GDP), and provided employment for over half of the population.

The economic strategies implemented in recent decades, such as industrialization, the promotion of a regional common market, and the introduction of "non-traditional" exports have not translated into a better quality of life for the vast majority of Guatemalans, as statistics and the virtual non-existence of basic infrastructure in many areas of the country prove. Although it is a regional leader in terms of macroeconomic indicators, in the 1990s the percentage of the Guatemalan population living

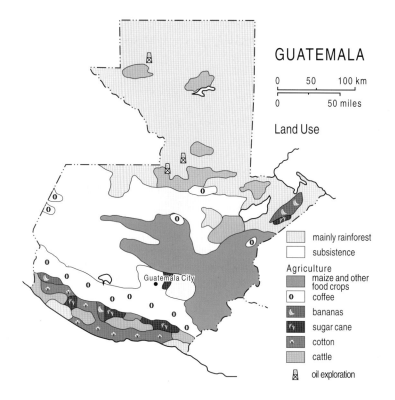

GUATEMALA

0   50   100 km

0   50 miles

Land Use

mainly rainforest

subsistence

Agriculture

maize and other food crops

o coffee

bananas

sugar cane

cotton

cattle

oil exploration

Guatemala City

in poverty increased. According to the government's planning office, at the beginning of the 1990s, 89 percent were poor, and 67 percent extremely poor. International agencies agree that more than half the population is still unable to meet their most basic food needs.

Guatemala has the region's highest GDP, but this wealth is very unevenly distributed. The poorest ten percent of the population take home 0.6 percent of the national income, while the richest ten percent pockets 46.6 percent. The country leads Central America in illiteracy (48 percent of the population), infant mortality (48 per 1,000), the lowest average infant birth weight, the lowest ratio of doctors per patient (one doctor for 4,000), and the lowest percentage of children enrolled in school. Even economists more concerned with macro-economic growth than with income distribution agree that investing in "human capital," mainly through education, is vital to economic development. The UN recommends that a minimum of five to seven percent of a country's GDP should be spent on education. In 1980, the Guatemalan government spent 2.4 percent of GDP, and in 1990, only 1.7 percent.

In all of the above categories the statistics are significantly worse for Mayans compared to Ladinos. Mayans live an average of sixteen years less than Ladinos due to poor nutrition and lack of access to health services. Only 39 percent of the Mayan population is literate, compared to 61 percent of Ladinos. 80 percent of indigenous people live in rural areas, where access to public services is very restricted, and 68 percent of the Mayan population works in agriculture. Not only did their wages decline during the 1980s, but Mayans earned only half of the average national wage. Even the sober reports of the World Bank note that "indigenous people in Guatemala are the poorest of the poor."

It's Good to Talk

In Guatemala City, well-heeled executives whip down the wide avenues in their Mercedes while doing business deals on their cellular phones. At home they cruise the Internet while their Maya *muchacha* (domestic worker) serves them a cocktail.

In Barillas, Huehuetenango, on the northwestern border with Mexico, a recently returned refugee walks eight hours and then travels an hour by bus to get to the nearest telephone to call a sister who is working in Los Angeles, California. He is not having a good day. The only phone for the population of eight districts, covering thousands of people, is not working. It has been raining heavily in the area and no one knows when the line will be up again. He could wait, and take the chance that the phone might be working in the morning, but he doesn't have enough money to pay for food and lodging in the town for the night and pay for the call. He begins the long, arduous journey back to his village.

In Guatemala in 1997 only two percent of the population had a telephone.

The Wealth of the Land

Guatemala's macroeconomic wealth has been based primarily on export crops and therefore land is the major source of wealth in Guatemala. In addition, it carries important cultural and religious meanings for the Maya. The gross inequality in land distribution is the single most important factor in the terrible poverty and quality of life in Guatemala. Approximately two thirds of Guatemalans live in rural areas, and over half of the economically active population work in agriculture. Nearly 90 percent of farms are too small to provide adequate subsistence, while two percent of farms use up 65 percent of land.

It is estimated that less than half of Guatemala's land is suitable for farming, with only 26 percent apt for agriculture and 21 percent for permanent pasture. Zones of land usage differ greatly. The humid southern coast, with the most fertile land in the country, is a huge expanse of cotton and sugar plantations, interspersed with groves of rubber trees and cattle ranches. In the colder highlands, where two thirds of the population live, most arable land is divided into small plots that crisscross mountainsides in a patchwork of beans, maize, and green vegetables. Some of the best land in the highlands belongs to large landowners who grow coffee and non-traditional crops.

The struggle over land ownership dates from colonial times. The unequal distribution of land was part of the process of conquest, during which the Spanish crown confiscated all land and redistributed it to its *conquistadores*. Some land was granted to indigenous communities, to allow them to subsist and provide forced labor. In the nineteenth century, indigenous peasants were deprived of much of this land by decree, to make way for the large coffee estates. Successive authoritarian governments continued to grant Mayan lands to national and international economic elites. As a result, many Mayans were deprived of even subsistence plots and forced to migrate seasonally to work on the plantations on the southern coast.

The Arbenz land reform of 1952 is the only time a Guatemalan government has attempted to change the pattern of land ownership to benefit the poor. The regimes which followed in the 1960s and 1970s preferred to open up areas of the Petén rainforest to landless peasants for cultivation, inviting ecological disaster, rather than redistributing fertile land suitable for farming.

To date the inequality in land distribution remains unsolved. The partial land reform began by Arbenz in 1952 led to the violent interference of the U.S. and ushered in thirty years of military dictatorship. It also fueled support for the guerrillas who organized to fight against the reversal of the reforms and the military's support of large landowners' interests. In the 1970s, the struggle for land became central to the civil war. Two decades later, some of the most active *campesino* organizations are those pushing for land reform. Some re-emerged after having gone underground during the military repression, such as the Committee for Campesino Unity (CUC). Others, like the National Indigenous and Campesino Co-ordination (CONIC), were created in the early 1990s.

In the peace process (see Chapter 2) the land question is treated in two of the accords, but land reform is not mentioned. The significant behind-the-scenes work of CACIF has meant that the agreements leave the issue of land ownership to market forces. In the socio-economic accord the government does agree to carry out a new registration of lands and revise ownership. This process could benefit indigenous communities which had their communal lands illegally confiscated, but it also brings to the fore land disputes between smallholders. The accord also mandates the creation of a bank, which can be help *campesinos* purchase land through a credit system in a long and drawn-out process.

Access to land - most houses have
their *milpa*, Zunil, Quetzaltenango

Robert Francis/
South American Pictures

One of the highest birth rates in Latin America combined with increasing ecological degradation means that land distribution is a more urgent issue now than ever. As a consequence, newspapers abound with reports of land conflicts and farm occupations. Meanwhile, plantation owners on the southern coast announced they were arming to defend their properties, while *campesino* organizations have stepped up their struggle.

Brewing Misery

The earthy-smelling brew the world wakes up to may conjure images of smiling peasants, playfully dropping their beans into a wicker basket on the verdant slopes of a cloud-topped volcano. Even in the most exclusive of gourmet shops, coffee costs less than a few dollars, and provides the simplest of pleasures. But the cost of cultivating coffee for most Guatemalans has been extraordinarily high. No other crop has so shaped the country's destiny.

The introduction of coffee to Guatemala in the mid-1800s led to coffee growers accumulating vast tracts of the most fertile land. The country's development and infrastructure were then geared to facilitate coffee cultivation. The first ports, railways, and roads were built to provide coffee to the U.S. and Europe, rather than with the country's long-term development needs in mind. Coffee reinforced the power of an entrenched and reactionary oligarchy, which was dependent on forced labor. Despite agricultural diversification, in the late 1990s, coffee continued to be the country's single most important export earner.

Taxing Times and International Aid

In addition to land reform, fair taxation would provide a way of redistributing wealth and ensuring basic services such as health and education for the majority. But historically, Guatemala has had one of the smallest tax bases in Latin America, never accounting for more than eight percent of GDP. The wealthy pay extremely low taxes, in keeping with their ability to influence state policy, thus making tax revenue the second lowest in the continent after Haiti. Not surprisingly, government spending is insufficient to even begin to tackle poverty in Guatemala.

The first Guatemalan president to introduce income tax legislation was Arbenz, who was overthrown days before the Congress was due to approve the bill. When civilian president Cerezo was elected in 1985, he also attempted a lukewarm tax reform and was met with at least two serious coup attempts and a general strike on the part of the business association, CACIF, which paralyzed the country and forced him to withdraw the bill. As a result of the historic failure to tax the wealthy, the state has not had enough income to both provide for the population's basic needs and support a large army. In the late 1990s, there were few public services in the countryside, and health services in urban areas were mostly private, or based on the modest social security system dating back to the Arbenz period. In the Cuchumatanes region near the Mexican border, villagers still had to walk up to three days to buy and sell produce, visit a doctor, or vote. Large areas of the country need roads and bridges to cross rivers that swell to several times their normal size during the rainy season. Gastrointestinal diseases and cholera recur due to the lack of a national potable water system.

The international community pledged US$1.9 billion in aid to Guatemala for the implementation of the Peace Accords, nearly matching export income for 1996. These funds are expected to alleviate rural poverty and provide for basic infrastructure. But the flow of international aid is conditional on the state raising US$700 million in taxes. At a meeting in September 1997, donors remarked on the slow pace of tax reform when the Guatemalan government complained of donor cash not being made available. The government claimed that revenue from taxes increased from seven to ten percent of GDP by the end of 1997. A major reason for this, however, was a dramatic increase in regressive taxes on goods and services which hit the poor much harder than the rich. There has been a marked slowdown in domestic demand, which is seen to be in part responsible for the reduced rate of growth of the economy.

A new revenues authority was created in 1998 to guarantee that the tax base is increased to twelve percent of GDP by the end of the millennium, but this will depend on doubtful political will. The new tax authority could deter corruption and tax evasion, and ensure that the wealthy contribute significantly, for the first time, to the economic development of the whole country.

The Private Sector

The engine of the Guatemalan economy is the private sector, which is historically one of the most conservative and intransigent business classes in Latin America. The old landowning oligarchy still controls traditional exports such as coffee and wields enormous political influence. They have created an economic climate in which free trade, low taxes and exploitation of labor are maintained, if necessary, by force. They have traditionally cooperated, sometimes uneasily, with the army, to ensure the protection of their interests, and between them they represent the main sectors in society opposing modernization, democratization, and even mild reforms to ameliorate the extreme poverty of the majority of Guatemalans.

The Guatemalan business class has always been more interested in the international market than in creating an internal market, which would require increasing wages to create consumers. Guatemalan entrepreneurs look to Miami, New York, and Los Angeles rather than the provincial capitals of Cobán, Huehuetenango, and Quetzaltenango, where outside the limited urban areas the majority of the population continues to live as they have for centuries.

But the economic elite is becoming less monolithic. There is a technocratic new wave of economic interests which supports electoral democracy and countenances limited reforms. Since the International Monetary Fund (IMF) recommended tax raises and an increased role for the state in education and health (a terrible indictment of Guatemalan services, given that the IMF's advice in the rest of Latin America has meant cuts in social spending), they have become reconciled to some degree of change. The modernizing wing of the private sector can be found in some of the newer export crops, such as sugar and non-traditionals, as well as in services such as banking. They are not separate from the traditional oligarchy, however, since many of the wealthiest families have diversified their interests into the newer ventures.

The sugar industry, for example, which in 1997 was the most dynamic sector of the agricultural economy, still relies on the concentration of land and manufacturing installations, in this case refineries, which benefits a small number of families. Owners are using new technology and working conditions are better than in other traditional agricultural sectors such as coffee. The sugar modernizers, however, are still dependent on protectionist state policies and fixed prices on the local market. Guatemalans must buy

Cutting cane, sugar plantation, Suchitepequez   *Paul Smith/PANOS Pictures*

the most expensive sugar in Central America and bankroll the state's subsidy of sugar production.

The private sector is well organized politically in a number of chambers of commerce and business associations. The most important associations belong to the Coordinating Committee of Agricultural, Commercial, Industrial and Financial Associations (CACIF). According to economists, CACIF represents over 80 percent of GDP, and wields more power than any political party in Guatemala. In terms of political parties, the "modernizing" wing of the private sector has expressed itself most successfully through the government of the National Advance Party (PAN) of President Arzú (1995-1999).

The unions in Guatemala are no match for the power of the private sector. Because of the legacy of violence against trade unions and social activists, less than five percent of the workforce in Guatemala is organized. On June 21, 1980, 31 union leaders were meeting in their offices in downtown Guatemala City when the building was surrounded by 60 armed men. Four union leaders managed to escape. The rest were never seen again. The only testimony to their presence that day were the bloodstains left on the walls of the meeting room on the second floor. Two months later, on August 24, 1980, seventeen more union leaders were disappeared while at a retreat center in the capital. A total of 45 union leaders were murdered within a two-month period in 1980, setting the union movement back a generation.

The nature of the Guatemalan economy also makes it difficult for workers to organize. In the mid-1990s only 34 percent of Guatemala's economically active population of three million were in formal employment. The rest were subsistence farmers, or worked in the informal sector. Many workers are forced to migrate seasonally to work on the southern plantations, or they hold down two or three different jobs in the informal sector. Unions became discredited in some quarters because they were associated with the broader left political struggle and the guerrillas, rather than with concrete gains in the workplace. But with the increase in political space since democratization, unions and federations of unions have begun to organize again and play a role in national politics. Labor organizations have also been affected by the introduction of *solidarismo*, a philosophy promoted by the Catholic Church and businesses to counter union organizing. Factory owners encourage the creation of joint financial associations, in which workers and management pool resources to form credit cooperatives and fund investment projects. *Solidarismo* has provided workers with material benefits, despite its anti-union nature.

The Media

Since almost half of the Guatemalan population is illiterate and many barely literate, the spoken word is still the most important form of communication. Even in the most remote mountain village, someone will have a radio, and this is the only truly nationwide media: there are 6.6 radios per 100 inhabitants while only two Guatemalans in 100 buy a daily newspaper. Numerous radio stations operate throughout the country, and many rural towns now have their own stations, often run by a local church, either Catholic or Protestant or one of each. In the mid-1990s, many local stations programming in Maya languages appeared.

There are four or five major newspapers published in Guatemala City, the number depending on the financial fortunes of the less-established papers. *Prensa Libre*, founded in 1951, is the only one distributed nationwide. The rest are read primarily in the capital and in a few of the larger cities and towns. Most of the newspapers are backed financially by a different sector of the economic elite, and the editorial line reflects and defends these interests. *Crónica* is the one major weekly news magazine worth reading, with interviews with government officials and other national personages.

Guatemalan newspapers are not famed for careful reporting of events (journalists are generally underpaid and overworked), but the editorials

Listening to radio Mam

Paul Smith

do give an idea of the scope of national debate. It is standard practice to accompany an editorial with a photograph of the writer, and a cursory review of these quickly demonstrates that Ladino men make up the majority of opinion makers.

Even for the urban population who buy a daily newspaper, the most important news of the day will probably come via *Guatebolas*, rather than the morning headlines. *Una bola* is Guatemalan slang for a rumor, but the word *bola* actually means a ball and is used in Spanish to refer to a snowball. Guatemalans in political circles joke about this common practice, which is used all too often to pass on false information. The *bola* snowballs with each teller, and a minor incident can become a full-blown conspiracy by the end of the working day. *Guatebolas* also operate at the level of local news and events in small villages, where repression has left its mark on people's ways of relating to each other. Until recently, a person who dared to be openly critical was courting torture and murder. *Bolas* provided a defense mechanism, since they passed on "information" from supposedly "anonymous" sources.

Yet the most notable characteristic of the Guatemalan media is its survival. The pursuit of a career as a serious journalist before 1985, and for some time after, was practically suicide. Between 1978 and 1985, 47 Guatemalan journalists were murdered and at least 100 fled into exile. In the 1980s, the offices of several news media were bombed, and bomb threats continued into the 1990s. Even in the mid-1990s, some journalists continued to receive anonymous death threats, and the relationship between the media and the government is not always easy.

The situation improved dramatically by the end of the 1990s. After the signing of the final peace accord, newspapers began publishing articles detailing the involvement of named military officials in criminal activity, a phenomenon impossible to imagine previously. There is no central government censorship board, and technically Guatemala has a "free press," but the legacy of four decades of repression and the murder of many journalists has led to a culture of self-censorship. Hope lies in a new generation of broadcasters and reporters whose formative experience has been the return to formal democracy rather than the horror of the early 1980s.

Women

Guatemala is a strongly patriarchal society, marked by the *machismo* present in most Latin American countries. But sexism is not the only form of discrimination. Race and class divide the category of "women" in Guatemala into very different realities for Maya and Ladino women. Maternal mortality underlines the differences in quality of life between women: of indigenous women, 22.5 die per 10,000 births, while for non-indigenous women the figure is 9.6 per 10,000 births. Life expectancy provides more stark proof: 48 years for Maya women, 65 for Ladinas. The terrible illiteracy statistics for Guatemala are worse for women in general, with 60 percent illiteracy for women compared to 37 percent for men, according to government figures. The breakdown for Maya women, with 72 percent illiteracy, is striking when compared to the 25 percent for Ladino women.

Women's status in Guatemalan law is contradictory. The Constitution of 1985 guarantees equality to men and women in all spheres of life. There are still laws in force dating to the Civil Code of 1877, however, which allow husbands to bar their wives from employment. The revised Civil Code of 1975 still has differing definitions of adultery for men and women. It was only in 1996 that Congress passed a law protecting women from physical and psychological violence in their homes. With regards to rights in the workplace, the Labor Code is written in paternalistic language and does not cover domestic work, which is an important source of employment for poor women in Guatemala.

Washing by hand, Quetzaltenango *Robert Francis/South American Pictures*

Despite double and triple work shifts in markets, fields, factories, offices, and homes, women earn only 13.8 percent of the national income. They constitute almost 40 percent of the working population in Guatemala City and are the majority in the informal sector. They also contribute significantly to agriculture, although their work in this sector has traditionally been unpaid.

Women's political participation was boosted in theory by their access to the vote in 1945. The Guatemalan Women's Alliance was also formed in the years of political opening between 1944-54. But the 1954 coup meant a return to the predominantly conservative and patriarchal values which still reign in Guatemalan society. Women came together whenever the political climate allowed it, but it was not until the Cerezo government (1986-91) that organizing became possible. Since then, a number of feminist organizations have appeared. A national network of women's groups is slowly extending into the countryside, and more information on the situation of women is being gathered.

In spite of the political constraints, it was women who founded the human rights organizations which began to work nationally and internationally against human rights violations in the 1980s. Although they do not have gender-specific aims, they have brought women into the political arena. For example, two high-profile leaders of human rights organizations are now members of parliament for the New Guatemalan

Democratic Front (FDNG): Rosalina Tuyuc of the National Coordination of Guatemalan Widows, (CONAVIGUA) and Nineth Montenegro, of the Mutual Support Group (GAM).

Development Alternatives for Whom?

As in the rest of Latin America, from the 1950s on, industrialization and import substitution were undertaken to reduce the dependency on agro-exports. But although Guatemala is the most industrialized country in Central America, the majority has benefited little from industry. Most of the rural poor who flood the marginal *barrios* of Guatemala City have not found jobs in the industrial sector. Many have ended up selling chewing gum, contraband clothing and cassettes, homemade candy, and an array of useless gadgets on the streets. In 1996, industry still represented only approximately fourteen percent of the GDP. Guatemalan industry involves primarily food processing, printing, chemicals, and the production of consumer goods such as clothing, shoes, tobacco, rum, and beer.

In the 1960s a Central American Common Market (CACM) was founded to promote industrialization and trade. The market collapsed partly due to the wars being fought throughout the region in the 1980s. One weakness of the common market was the lack of land reform and the unmet need to create and expand national markets. There were not enough consumers with buying power in Central America to sustain the fledgling market, and the governments in turn were not interested in promoting policies such as fair wages in order to create consumers. In 1996, the minimum wage in Guatemala was 15.95 quetzales ($2.70) daily for agricultural workers, and 17.60 quetzales ($2.96) in the non-agricultural sector. Although El Salvador, Costa Rica and Honduras buy 24.5 percent of Guatemala's exports, in the mid-1990s the U.S. continues to be Guatemala's most important trading partner. The U.S. buys 36 percent of Guatemalan exports, and many McDonald's hamburgers are made with Guatemalan beef.

Non-traditional exports were introduced in the 1960s to contribute to diversification. The heart of the strategy was to capitalize on Guatemala's one increasing resource and so-called "comparative advantage": the cheap and abundant labor force. Producers began growing broccoli and snow peas, melons, and flowers to sell to the U.S., Europe, and Japan. Other non-traditionals include sesame, shrimp, fish, lobster, fresh and processed fruits and wood. Non-traditional exports generally require a higher level of technology and inputs than the majority of small peasant farmers can afford, such as refrigeration, information on specialized markets, quick transport, fertilizers, and pesticides. Environmental groups have criticized the dependence of non-traditionals on chemical fertilizers and pesticides, and pointed out the related land exhaustion. They warn that the model is unsustainable.

Maquiladora factories have also been promoted as a modernizing alternative source of employment. The *maquila* industry began in the mid-1980s, mostly with foreign capital. Investors were attracted to Guatemala by cheap labor and special tax-free zones. In the mid-1990s there were an estimated 225 factories operating in Guatemala. Most of the 70,000 workers are women, who are preferred by employers because they are seen as passive, hard-working and easily intimidated. Employers know that many women support families on their average wage of $1.25 per hour, and yet they pay women less than men, arguing that they are not the "main" wage earners. For many women, alternative employment is scarce, traditionally in domestic service, where wages are lower and conditions often more demeaning.

Early in the 1990s, Korean-owned *maquilas* made international headlines because of labor abuses. Working conditions in the *maquila* tend to be exploitative, with many women working twelve and thirteen-hour days, with supervised three-minute toilet breaks. Pregnant women are often fired, as are those who try to organize unions. The *maquilas* produce for some of the biggest brand names sold in the U.S., including Nike, Sears, Calvin Klein, Levi-Strauss and Wrangler. The U.S. market consumes 90 percent of Guatemala's *maquila*-made goods.

Tourism, Drugs and Migration

As Norman Lewis observed in his novel, *The Volcanoes Above Us* (1957), "For anyone who has lived in Guatemala, other countries, by contrast, are lacking in savor. The problem confronting the people who want to promote a prosperous tourist industry is how to take out this over-strong flavor so that only the safely picturesque remains. This is difficult in a country which lies under the shadow of 32 volcanoes..."

The "over-strong flavor" no longer seems to be a deterrent to foreign visitors, as tourism has become a major income earner after coffee exports, bringing in US$296 million in 1997. According to the Guatemalan Tourism Institute, in 1995, over half a million tourists from all over the world visited the country. Many Guatemalan businessmen are setting their hopes on eco-tourism as a new source of revenue. But because of the increasing criminal violence, which has replaced the political violence of the past, tourism has proved to be as vulnerable an economic venture as non-traditional exports. Common crime increased in 1997, particularly kidnappings and muggings, and foreign tourists have been the target of petty theft and physical violence. The signing of a final peace accord in neighboring El Salvador in 1990 was followed by an increase in crime in that country, with thousands of former soldiers and ex-guerrillas, many still with guns, out of work. A similar pattern seems to be emerging in post-war Guatemala.

During the 1980s, drugs became one of Guatemala's new "unofficial" non-traditional exports. According to press reports and the U.S. Drug Enforcement Agency (DEA), Guatemala became an important opium producer and marijuana grower, and a trans-shipment point for cocaine on its way to the United States. Guatemalan authorities estimated that 85 percent of crime in 1996 was related to drug trafficking, which was controlled by some 600 gangs. The end of the war has meant a large number of unemployed and discontented former soldiers turning to crime, as well as military involvement at higher levels in the lucrative drugs commerce. A significant amount of organized crime is thought to be connected to the military. The number of gang members and their expertise were probably boosted by the U.S. crackdown on immigration in 1998, which meant the deportation of many Guatemalans living in the Los Angeles area.

Guatemalans living in *El Norte* (literally the North, meaning the U.S.) sent home nearly US$350 million in 1995 according to the Bank of Guatemala, making it another important source of revenue. Some economists believe that the countless money orders sent from Los Angeles, Chicago and other U.S. cities to relatives in even the most remote areas surpass national income from coffee exports. This economic safety valve could disappear in the late 1990s with the end of the civil war, when thousands of Guatemalans in the U.S. might have their political asylum status revoked.

The option of heading north has had a great cultural and economic impact on rural Guatemala. Rather than heading south for seasonal work in the plantations, many Maya now prefer to head north to work in textile factories, restaurants, and other menial jobs. The money they send home changes social patterns in rural Guatemala. Mayan elders also complain that many of the youth who go north are *maleados*, or "ruined," by the influence of American culture. They leave wearing some vestige of their native clothing and return in Levi's and Nike's.

The Environment

Known as the land of "eternal spring," Guatemala is famed for its temperate climate and varied flora. It is one of the most fertile and biologically diverse countries in Latin America. The country divides into distinct geographical areas: the southern lowlands along the Pacific coast, which lie at the feet of a mainly volcanic mountain chain, the temperate central highlands, the hot tropical Caribbean east coast, and the dense tropical forests of Petén to the north, on the border of Mexico and Belize.

Guatemala is part of a World Bank initiative to create a Central American "ecological corridor" that would run from Mexico to Panama. The presidents of the region agreed to its creation in 1994. Guatemala also shares with Mexico and Belize the *Selva Maya* (Mayan Jungle), which comprises the lowland rainforests that surround many of the best-known Classical Mayan ruins. It is the largest area of rainforest north of the Amazon. But despite the creation of conservation areas, such as the *Biósfera Maya* (Mayan Biosphere) in 1990, the threats to the survival of the forest are numerous.

The military-supported development of the north and northeast which began in the 1960s included concessions to foreign companies to prospect for oil and minerals. In addition to the intensive resource exploitation, their development plans led to violence as the army used force against the indigenous population to assert control over the "new frontier." The military government of the time claimed it was opening up the area to landless *campesinos* from other parts of Guatemala. The main beneficiaries, however, have been wealthy ranchers, among them army officers, who were granted large extensions of land mainly for cattle grazing. The majority of beef produced is for export, priced beyond the means of most Guatemalans. The expansion of beef production actually contributed to a 50 percent drop in national beef consumption.

The loss of the forest has accelerated greatly with the expansion of cattle ranching. Today Guatemala's forest cover is down to between 27 and 42 percent of the national territory, from 77 percent in 1960. At the present rate of deforestation, it will only take another 30 or so years before the forest is gone. There are grave effects for the agricultural potential of the land due to the effect of deforestation: soil erosion and leaching mean that it is calculated that up to 40 percent of Guatemala's agricultural land has lost its productive capacity.

According to the government office responsible for the Biósfera Maya, Guatemala suffers from some of the most rapid deforestation in the world, with nearly 600 square miles cut down each year. The Petén rainforest is often in the news because poor landless *campesinos* have occupied land in environmentally protected zones there, as the result of inadequate land distribution policies. While the army is sent in to forcefully evict *campesinos*, government officials look the other way as some military officers, wealthy landowners and foreign companies ship out precious woods by the truckload. In the meantime, it is the same wealthy ruling elites in the government who portray Guatemala as a haven for eco-tourism. While the reality is deforestation, the marketing strategies make use of the Quetzal, the now practically extinct national bird, to attract tourists to the fast-diminishing rainforests. There is no real commitment to investment in conservation or sustainable practices in managing the remaining forests.

For the many environmental organizations set up in Guatemala since the 1980s it seems clear that there is a strong link between the problems of land use associated with a skewed distribution and the ecological degradation of Guatemala's natural resources. Indigenous people have also pointed out that environmental destruction is part of a wider move to destroy their way of life in the name of commercial progress, at the cost of their lives and land.

4   RELIGION AND CULTURE: THE MAYA DAWN

Religious Diversity

Guatemala is officially a Catholic country, as it has been for five centuries, although in fact there is religious diversity. The Catholic faith was part of the conquest process, but the clouds of incense and colorful Easter week processions which attract tourists and jam city streets mask the many manifestations of religion in Guatemala. In the cold highlands, indigenous priests have kept Mayan spirituality alive through ancient ceremonies, jealously guarding their sacred places. In towns and throughout the countryside, evangelical sects have also increased dramatically in the past two decades.

A key way in which the Maya resisted the Spanish conquest was by preserving their own rites and customs within Catholic ritual. This process of "syncretism" has always been present and has challenged the Catholic clergy. Thomas Gage, a priest assigned to the small parish of Amatitlán in the early 1600s wrote despairingly: "Many are given to witchcraft, and are deluded by the devil to believe that their life dependeth upon the life of such and such a beast which they take unto them as their familiar spirit...commonly a buck, doe, lion, tiger, dog or eagle...they yield unto the worshipping of Saints' images because they look upon them as much like their Forefathers' idols, and think verily those saints were of their opinion, and that those beasts were their familiar spirits..."

Syncretism in Santiago Atitlán and Maximón

The dark church with its three-feet thick walls is one of the oldest on the continent, and a modern sign of syncretism. Inside, more than 50 large wooden statues of saints line the walls, all wrapped in colorful indigenous scarves and dressed in the *traje* typical of Santiago. Some saints weep, hands outstretched, others bleed from painted wounds, while Mayan women kneel at the altar and loudly lament a poor harvest, a husband's drinking, a stillborn child.

Next to the church is a tiny square chapel that comes alive every Easter week. It is the home of Maximón, a local maize god who loves to drink and smoke. Legend has it that centuries ago, Maximón was a man who offered to take care of all the women in Santiago Atitlán while the men went to till their fields. The men came home one evening to find Maximón in bed with their wives, and so they cut off his arms and legs in revenge. Maximón became a god, and today is represented by a wooden mask fixed on a body made up of layer after layer of shiny colored scarves. Every Easter week Maximón holds court in his special chapel while hundreds of locals and tourists visit to ask him to grant a wish, plying him with cigars and rum.

The Catholic Church

The Catholic Church remains one of the major pillars of power in Guatemala, along with the private sector and the army. Statements made by Catholic bishops criticizing government policy make national headlines, and the Church runs social services, private schools, and a major university.

The church's power has cyclically waxed and waned since the conquest, depending on its alliances with the state. It was a powerful institution until the nineteenth century, providing Spaniards with a justification for domination in order to "save the souls" of the heathen Maya. The situation changed in 1871 when the Liberal government confiscated church lands, introduced secular education and opened the country to Protestant missionaries.

It was not until the Ubico dictatorship of the 1930s that the church regained some of its power. It tried to recover the ground lost in the countryside through an organization called Catholic Action. Catholic Action catechists advocated a more orthodox Catholicism than the mixture of Mayan spirituality and Catholic rite which had evolved in many rural areas. In the 1950s and 1960s, the organization moved from evangelism into politics, becoming part of the Church's anti-Communist campaign. By the 1970s, however, contact with the rural poor had radicalized many Catholic activists and clergy, who became more concerned with social development than salvation.

The shift from saving souls to saving lives had terrible consequences. Many catechists, along with other progressive activists in the highlands, were killed by the army. Foreign clergy were expelled from the country, and churches closed down in some war zones. Some churches in Quiché were occupied by the army and used as torture chambers during this period. In the meantime, the hierarchy of the Church remained conservative and on excellent terms with the army and economic elite.

In 1983, the hierarchy finally caught up politically with the priests and nuns in the field with the appointment of a progressive Archbishop, Próspero Penados del Barrio. In 1988 the bishops issued a Pastoral Letter entitled *The Clamor for Land* which was a strong indictment of the unjust distribution of land as the root of the country's social problems. The bishops demanded radical reforms to redistribute land, as well as the protection of *campesino* organizations and respect for their human rights. Throughout the 1990s, the social vocation of the Catholic Church was demonstrated in its pioneering work defending human rights, through the Archbishops' Human Rights Office (ODHA). The Bishop's Conference has been a prominent promoter of social justice and active in the peace process and refugee returns.

A religious procession during the annual fiesta, Santa Lucia de la Reforma, Totonicapán

Paul Smith

An important change within the Catholic Church during the 1980s and 1990s was the acceptance of Mayan religious practices. In the western department of Huehuetenango, in the 1950s and 1960s American Maryknoll missionaries would stamp out candles lit outside the church and forbid other traditional Mayan practices. By the 1990s, several priests in the same area were local Huehuetecos. Their ancestors were Mayan priests, so they respect Mayan spirituality and see their beliefs as complementary to Catholicism. The Catholic clergy in Guatemala has historically been dominated by foreigners, but today one third of the priests in training are indigenous, as well as Guatemalan.

Protestant Expansion

In 1980, the sixteenth-century Catholic cathedral in the small town of Santiago Atitlán was the most important center for religious activity. By the 1990s, the town had Evangelical churches on many street corners, and on any night of the week these popular tourist spots reverberate with hundreds of Tzutuhiles singing Evangelical hymns to the strumming of electric guitars, with the sound of voices speaking in tongues in the background.

Many cultural, economic and political factors have contributed to the spread of Evangelical churches. Historically, there has been an openness to Protestant missionaries since the end of the nineteenth century, when a

U.S. Presbyterian mission arrived, invited by the President of Guatemala himself. The Catholic Church had failed to meet the spiritual needs of the Mayan population, and many priests did not learn indigenous languages. In contrast, the Protestants and Evangelicals rapidly began publishing the Bible in several indigenous languages and distributing it for free.

Another important cultural factor is that Evangelical sects generally discourage the use of alcohol. Alcohol is a serious problem in many rural villages where some men often drink the little income they receive from selling their crops. Many women are greatly relieved when their husbands join an Evangelical church, since the Catholic Church never seriously addressed this social problem. The elitism of the Catholic Church and its hierarchical nature have also contributed to the growth of Evangelism. While it takes years of study and often considerable financial resources for a Mayan to become a Catholic priest, virtually any community leader with charisma can become a local Evangelical pastor.

Evangelical and Protestant churches in general have made an important contribution in terms of social services and meeting the material needs of rural Guatemalans. Presbyterians built Guatemala's first hospital, and Evangelicals have built numerous schools and health clinics, and administered food programs in rural areas. Some denominations organize yearly visits of foreign delegations of doctors and other professionals who provide services free of charge to Guatemalans.

The Evangelical churches began to flourish during the repression of the early 1980s. The ascendance of Evangelical General Ríos Montt to the presidency in 1982 was a sign to many that to convert from Catholicism to Evangelism could literally mean physical salvation. Ríos Montt's highly authoritarian, black-and-white view of the world, characteristic of Evangelical oratory, also appealed to many Guatemalans. His presidency opened the door for conservative Evangelical sects from the U.S.

The Protestant and Evangelical churches do not constitute one block politically. The traditional Protestant churches which have been in Guatemala the longest, the Presbyterians, Methodists, and Church of the Nazarene, tend to be more progressive and occasionally have allied with Catholic counterparts on issues such as human rights and the peace process. The newer Evangelical sects, on the other hand, can rarely unify to make public statements as a sector, due to the competition between the vast number of denominations. In general, though, they are extremely conservative, and either frown on any "left"-leaning political activities, or encourage a right-wing activism to combat what they view as "the devil's handiwork." President Jorge Serrano (1992-1993), forced out of power

Evangelical Christian rally, Guatemala City   *Paul Smith/PANOS Pictures*

after he attempted an auto-coup, was an influential member of a powerful Evangelical sect, and an example of this right-wing religious activism.

The Politics of Culture and Identity

Culture and identity were given a framework by the Peace Accord on the Identity and Rights of Indigenous People, signed in 1995, which defines Guatemalan society as: "multi-ethnic, pluri-cultural and multilingual." It would be too simplistic to divide Guatemala into a country of only Maya and Ladinos. Among the Maya, there are at least 21 different ethnic groups, of which the largest is the Quiché, (886,900 people) followed by the Mam and Kakchiquel (both about 440,000 people). Other recognized ethnic minorities include the Xinca, who are indigenous non-Maya, and the Garífuna, African-Guatemalans living on the Caribbean coast of the country. In addition, there are many Guatemalans of mixed ancestry who do not identify with a particular ethnic group and refer to themselves simply as "Guatemalan." There are also white Guatemalans of direct European descent who refer to themselves either as Guatemalan or white. Through simple observation of urban life in the newspapers and on television, an outsider is immediately aware that it is this last group that still holds the real political and economic power in this country.

Many refer to "apartheid" Guatemala because of the prevailing discrimination against the majority Mayan population. Racism is the legacy of the strict boundaries drawn during the colonial period. Spaniards born in the New World were known as *criollos* and as the centuries passed, *criollos* could be identified not only on the basis of Spanish descent but also by the ownership of large expanses of land and access to forced labor. The *criollos* formed the oligarchy which in many ways continues to dominate Guatemala. Midway in the social hierarchy were Ladinos, (originally Spanish-speaking Indians) who provided labor and overseers for the plantations. *Criollos* would employ Ladinos to do the dirty work of keeping the *indios* in order. In time, and particularly after the 1871 reforms, many Ladinos began to acquire land and wealth. The term *indio*, still used by many Ladinos to describe the Maya, continues to carry racist connotations in Guatemala.

The colonial period spawned two worlds — the Guatemala of forced labor and domination for the indigenous majority, and the Guatemala of wealth and privilege for those of Spanish descent. The beautiful tourist attraction, Antigua, just 40 minutes from Guatemala City, is an example of these two Guatemalas living side by side. Burgundy bougainvillea sets off the cream stucco walls of expansive colonial homes which now house some of Guatemala's loveliest cafes and restaurants. Those who built the homes, cobbled the quaint streets, and planted the fine gardens came from 28 indigenous villages surrounding the small city. When the conquerors first arrived and founded Antigua as the colonial capital of Central America, they hunted villagers at night to provide themselves with a labor force.

Although it is tempting to categorize the population into the right "identity box," in fact, the terms of each "identity" are not fixed, and change over time. The term Ladino has evolved since colonial times, when it referred to indigenous people who were not connected to communal lands, and is now known as the prevailing national culture. Likewise, the pan-Maya identity which is being redrawn in the "Maya Dawn" (see p.70) is a recent development, since historically there have been many community and municipality-based ethnic identities, with language as a defining marker of larger Mayan groups.

Estimates of the percentage of the population who are indigenous vary widely. Figures taken from the national census are partial, as "indigenous" is defined only with regard to traditional dress and language use. According to this data, 44 percent of the population is indigenous. Mayan leaders calculate the figure to be 65 percent, while academics compromise at half the population. Another source of debate are the numbers of Maya who have abandoned their *traje* and language, many of whom live in urban

GUATEMALA

The vegetable market,
Chichicastenango
Robert Francis/South American Pictures

BUYING AND SELLING
IN GUATEMALA
Ancient and modern markets
contribute to the country's
commerce.

Selling woven
goods, Sololá
Julio Etchart/Reportage

Downtown
Guatemala City
Sean Sprague

LAND AND MAIZE

Growing maize, living on the land, remain the occupations of the majority of Guatemalans.

The gods made the first Maqya-Quices out of clay. Few survived. They were soft, lacking strength; they fell apart before they could walk.

Then the gods tried wood. The wooden dolls talked and walked but were dry; they had no blood or substance, no memory and no purpose. They didn't know how to talk to the gods, or couldn't think of anything to say to them.

Then the gods made mothers and fathers of corn. They moulded their flesh with yellow and white corn.

The women and men of corn saw as much as the gods. Their glance ranged over the whole world. The gods breathed on them and left their eyes forever clouded, because they didn't want people to see over the horizon.

Popol Vuh, The religious book of the Mayas. Quoted in Eduardo Galeano, *Memory of Fire*.

A highland farmer examines his maize crop
Chris Sharp/South American Pictures

Working in the fields, Ixcán Grande, Quiché
Paul Smith/PANOS Pictures

Grinding maize
Paul Smith

Making tortillas
Paul Smith/PANOS Pictures

Drying maize on the roof, Zunil,
Quetzaltenango
Paul Smith/PANOS Pictures

The refugees return ...
"The man of maize returns to
build his country"
Gail Deutsch/PANOS Pictures

RELIGIOUS DIVERSITY
Public and private worship include indigenous beliefs
and Catholic rites in a rich syncretism.

Burning incense on the steps of
Santo Tomás
Martin Adler/PANOS Pictures

An Easter procession moves over a
road covered in colored sawdust
Robert Francis/South American Pictures

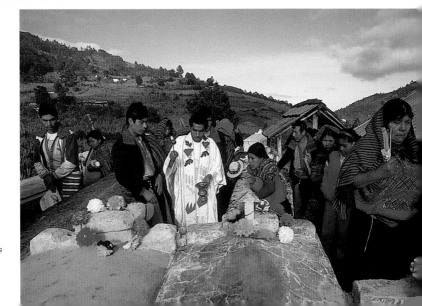

A Catholic
priest
blesses
graves on
the Day of
the Dead
*Paul Smith/
PANOS Pictures*

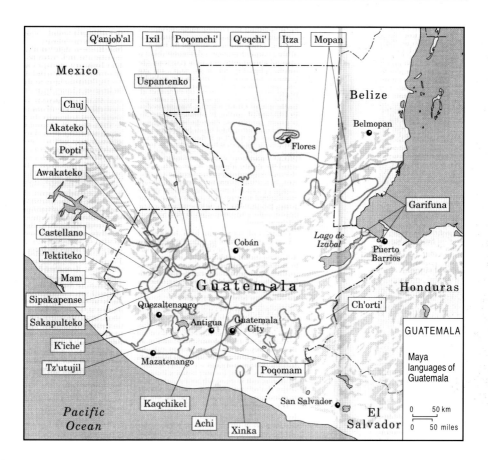

Source: Ministry of Education, Guatemala

centers, and who have become "ladinized." It is impossible to quantify how many Maya are affected by the cultural, economic, and educational factors which encourage or force individuals to integrate into the dominant Ladino culture. Of crucial importance is how people identify themselves.

The Indigenous Accord has provided an opportunity for the two predominant cultures within Guatemala to reassess how they relate to each other. Changes are to be made to the Constitution so the rights and identity of indigenous peoples will be recognized and respected "within the unity of the nation and the indivisibility of the Guatemalan state territory." This last phrase pre-empts claims to Maya autonomy. Instead, the government agrees to promote the "regionalization" of state services, particularly education and health, giving local Mayan authorities more control.

A Maya Doctor

Leticia Velazquez, a 34-year-old Quiché woman, was the only Mayan of 1,600 medical students at the San Carlos State University to graduate in 1991. Throughout her seven years of studies Velazquez suffered constant harassment and discrimination from teaching staff, some of whom tried unsuccessfully to expel her from the school. One doctor ordered her to cut off her braids. Her biggest problem was that she refused to change her traditional Mayan *traje*, an ankle-length woven skirt and embroidered blouse, for western wear.

"I have always been a bit of a rebel and thought that if I changed my clothes I would not be myself. So I resisted. It was when I went to the hospital to treat patients that the problems started. A resident doctor who was Ladino said to me, "Look, the way you're dressed shows a lack of respect for your patients. Please come in civilian clothes." I told him, "These are my civilian clothes. And besides it's not a lack of respect because I'm the doctor here and the patients have to learn to respect me. I'm indigenous and there are thousands and thousands of us who have more right than you to be working in this hospital."

After that he was very hard on me in the class and if I made a mistake he would say that I should be shining shoes in the park or planting onions instead of studying medicine."

Velazquez's struggle to overcome racism did not end with her graduation. In her first job at the same university, as the only Mayan in the office, she earned less than half of what her two Ladino colleagues in the same position received. Since then Velazquez has been recognized internationally as an expert in public health in indigenous communities and has worked to reform the Guatemalan health system.

"When I see how far I've come, I can't believe how I could have put up with so much. Now there are many more Maya in the university than before, but it's a slow process, and discrimination continues. One must be very clear about what is going on. Sometimes it seems as if they are paying attention to you, but then it turns out that you are just being used. Indigenous people are now "in fashion" and so Ladinos have to employ us, but often without real participation or power."

The Maya Dawn

According to Maya prophesies in the *Chilam Balam*, one of the most important Maya sacred texts, and based on calculations of the Mayan calendar, in 1987 one cycle of a long night ended and another cycle called the "new dawn" began. The "new dawn" is generally understood as a cultural revival, and it has coincided with the return to formal democracy in the 1980s, and the peace negotiations in the 1990s.

Since the return to democracy in 1986, a space opened to allow the Maya to organize. As part of the human rights movement described in Chapter 2, and as victims of the rural violence, the Maya have provided the social base for the new social and political organizations. Late in the 1980s, specifically Mayan organizations began to form, formulating ethnic demands and emphasizing the importance of a cultural revival and the struggle against racism.

The defense of Mayan languages has been an important rallying point of identity. One of the greatest recent gains was the state's recognition of indigenous languages and the potential impact on education, the justice system, and state services in general. The Academy of Mayan Languages was legally recognized by Congress in 1990. Eventually all teachers in Mayan areas should be bilingual, and children taught in their mother tongue as well as Spanish. In the past many children were punished by Ladino teachers for speaking anything other than Spanish, and made to feel ashamed of their language. A general educational reform is planned to give indigenous communities a role in proposing a curriculum that reflects their culture and values.

The fact that over twenty Mayan languages are still spoken in Guatemala today is testimony to the resistance of the Maya to Spanish culture, as is the continued use of *traje*. In most areas, Mayan men have adopted western clothing and only Mayan women still wear their long *corte* (skirt) and *huipil* (blouse). However, there are still some municipalities where the men proudly wear *traje,* such as Santiago Atitlán, Todos Santos, and San Juan Atitlán. By 1992, there were approximately 200 organizations working on Mayan issues, with both Mayan members and staff. A dozen magazines and publications were circulating Mayan issues and debates, and by the late 1990s some mainstream media were beginning to include Mayan contributors.

Mayan communities have survived for 500 years because of deeply rooted spiritual beliefs and traditions. The Mayan belief system, or *cosmovisión,* as they describe it, emphasizes the cyclical nature of history and importance of prophecy. So although they may have suffered for centuries, the certainty of a revival has carried many through the hardest of times.

Another factor which has helped the Maya to endure is the hermetic nature of many communities. This dates back to the colonial era when problems were resolved within the community rather than encouraging Spanish authorities to intervene. Communities protect their traditions and way of life by keeping them from outsiders, and shrouding them in secrecy. There is a strong emphasis on the collective rather than the individual. The most important unit for the Maya is his or her community, which often means one's village or municipality. Land is also fundamental to Mayan culture. One's land is where ancestors are buried, where one's history is maintained, and where the maize is grown generation after generation, ensuring the continuity of this maize-based culture.

Despite the threats that western culture and changing economic circumstances present to Mayan ways, each Mayan community continues to be a world unto itself. Villages may have their own laws and an intricate network of authorities, both political and spiritual, which have little to do with legally recognized state structures.

Indigenous Forms of Power

The type of authority within indigenous communities varies from one region to another, and in many areas these networks were gravely affected by the 36-year-long war. Some of the institutions which can still be found are:

The *cofradía,* originally a religious lay brotherhood within the Catholic Church, was adapted by the Maya into a political organization of elders which passes on traditional Mayan beliefs and community values. The *cofradía* is made up of men in a village or town who take care of their patron saint. They organize the festivities to honor their saints, and are also responsible for the physical care of the images, ensuring they are properly worshipped. In many places the *cofradía* became an important parallel religious power that challenged or kept in check the authority of the local priest. Membership implies social prestige and respect.

The Council of Elders is a group which often serves as the judicial body, which exercises customary law (see p.73) and discusses all matters of importance to the community. They are highly respected by the community and expected to provide a model of conduct.

Aj Q'ijab' or spiritual guides are men and women who know how to use herbs for healing, and who are the keepers of the Mayan calendar. They carry out community or social work, giving advice and consoling those in need. As keepers of the calendar, they are frequently consulted for the right date to hold ceremonies to mark events such as the harvest. Midwives and herbalists are usually older women who provide health services and charge what the patient can afford to pay. They are often the only local health resource in the most isolated rural areas where infant and maternal mortality is high.

These traditional Mayan authorities survive alongside the recognized municipal and village mayors. The village mayor, who is chosen by the community for one year, represents the village before the Guatemalan state and is an important figure in some areas. There are also a variety of minor unpaid posts in the Maya hierarchy, depending on the community's needs, such as messenger boy, postman, and keeper of the communal forest (where there is one left), all of which are considered ways into the *cofradía*.

The Mayan Legal System: Customary Law

Mayan structures of power within many villages and municipalities include ways of dealing with community problems, ranging from petty crime to major conflicts arising from land disputes and even homicide. This system of law is called *costumbre* or customary law.

Costumbre has survived and endured because of the non-existence of state institutions in many rural areas. Where the state does maintain a presence, and there is a judge, frequently neither he nor his clerks speak the local language, and cases can take years to resolve. The Guatemalan justice system was set up by and for Ladinos, and has historically discriminated against the Maya. Corruption is also rampant, and for many Maya going to the official legal system means aggravating and prolonging the problem.

Customary law is not a codified system like western legal systems, with set rules and punishments for certain crimes, but a flexible system that adapts and changes with the times, according to the type of crime or problem, and the individuals involved. It is based on the idea of restoring social harmony in the community, a kind of win-win strategy, rather than simply punishing the perpetrator of the crime. The way of resolving petty crime in a community, such as the theft of a farm animal, would vary depending on what was stolen, why it was stolen, who stole it, and how the victim was affected by the theft. Since most of the communities are tiny, the western concepts of investigating a crime and "innocent until proven guilty" can often be irrelevant as the person responsible is easily identified in a small village where everyone is poor, and the sudden acquisition of an item is easily noticed.

In Mayan communities the concept of restitution, paying back the victim and confessing to the crime, is much more important than a punishment such as sending the person to jail. To jail the person responsible is seen as ineffective, since he or she will be unable to work, which will have negative consequences for their family and impede their ability to pay back the victim.

While this system can be effective, it should not be idealized. The violence of the 1980s greatly altered the status quo in many Mayan communities, when the army imposed paramilitary authorities over existing ones. Civil patrolmen and military commissioners replaced the elders, and wielded extraordinary power, literally of life and death. Although these paramilitary networks were officially dismantled in the mid-1990s as part

Rigoberta Menchú Tum

Paddy Donnelly

of the peace process, in some communities the ex-patrolmen continue to exercise undue influence.

The principal problem with this parallel legal system is that it rests on the integrity of the local traditional authorities, and the respect of the community for them. Customary authorities can be ineffectual or manipulated against a member of the community to protect particular interests. They can also support prevailing cultural norms such as those which condone domestic violence.

Rigoberta Menchú Tum

Rigoberta Menchú is an internationally known Mayan leader, who works for the promotion of human rights and social justice. She received the Nobel Peace prize in 1992, the youngest ever recipient, as well as the first indigenous person to receive such recognition.

Her triumphant return to Guatemala in October 1992 with the award was welcomed with fireworks by the Maya, and deep resentment on the part of the Ladino government and establishment. Although she was awarded medals by other governments and honored at banquets hosted by heads of state, the President of her own country, Jorge Serrano, did not even attend the diplomatic reception in her honor. "He has an earache," was what his wife, who came in his stead, told the press. It was easy enough to believe that his ears hurt after the phone call informing him that a Mayan Indian had just been given the Nobel Prize.

Rigoberta Menchú was born in 1959 in the village of Chimel, in a Maya Quiché community. She worked from childhood, first in the fields and then as a domestic worker in Guatemala City. Her father was a peasant organizer who was killed in the Spanish embassy in 1980, along with others protesting the violence of the army in the countryside. Other close relatives, including brothers and her mother, were tortured and killed by the armed forces. She was forced into exile to Mexico in 1980. In 1983 a testimonial book about her life was published, entitled *I, Rigoberta Menchú*, followed in 1998 by *Crossing the Borders*, the continuation of her biography.

As well as her international work, she works in Guatemala through the Rigoberta Menchú Tum Foundation which carries out social and advocacy work in the areas of human rights, particularly for indigenous people. She has also been a long-time representative of the Committee for Campesino Unity (CUC).

Literature

Guatemala has a rich tradition of literature that shows how the diverse cultures have evolved and related. The country has inspired foreign writers such as Aldous Huxley and Eduardo Galeano, and produced several outstanding writers, many of whom have been forced to live in exile for considerable periods of time.

Guatemala's best known writer is Miguel Angel Asturias (1899-1974), who was awarded the Nobel Prize for Literature in 1967. He studied Mayan languages in Paris and anthropology at the *Musee de L'Homme* and in 1927 helped to translate the *Popol vuh* into French. His novels departed from the realism current at the time in other Indianist writers and instead he used myth to explore modern truths. In *Hombres de Maiz* (Men of Maize), his most famous novel, he uses Mayan myths to explore the conditions under which indigenous people lose not only their possessions but also their identity in contemporary Guatemala. Current Mayan intellectuals are critical of his portrayal, disagreeing with the assimilationist views he expounded elsewhere. He also wrote a novel about the nightmarish world of the Ubico dictatorship in *El Señor Presidente* (The President).

In *Hombres de Maiz*, the first myth-figure in the novel is Gaspar Ilóm, "an Indian chief of the old type, completely identified with his land, able to communicate with plants, animals and the earth, which are as sentient as himself." Miguel Angel Asturias' son, Rodrigo Asturias, whose *nom de guerre* is Gaspar Ilóm, is the head of ORPA (Revolutionary Organization of the People in Arms), one of the four organizations which make up the URNG. He is currently the Head of Communications for the political party which the URNG is forming. His political future was thrown into doubt in 1997, when he was implicated in a guerrilla kidnapping of an elderly woman from a prominent family.

The contemporary scene is replete with excellent writers, some based in Guatemala, others living in the U.S. Francisco Morales Santos, one of the most prominent poets, combines historical and social analysis as well as fiction in his poetry, as Victor Perera does in prose. Internationally, perhaps the best known novelist is the half-Guatemalan Francisco Goldman, whose first novel, *The Long Night of the White Chickens* (1992) won international acclaim. In 1995, *A Mayan Life: A Birth in the Village* was published, claiming to be the first novel written by a Mayan writer, Gaspar Pedro Gonzalez, although Mayan-identified poets, such as Humberto

Marimba band, Rabinal   *Sean Sprague*

Ak'abal, abound. The resurgence of Mayan culture means new voices are coming to the fore and this overview will soon expand into a great many names.

Music

The Maya are adept at assimilating foreign elements into their culture and music is thought to have played an important part in the conversion of the Maya to Catholicism. When the Spanish imposed their god and rituals, they forbade the Maya to worship their own deities and use their traditional rites. But they discovered that through the Maya's love of music, they could be persuaded to take up aspects of Catholicism. As religious syncretism arose from the collision of Mayan and Catholic beliefs, so was a new range of musical expression created.

Even today, traditional music is associated with religious ritual and faith. Rattles, drums, and many types of flutes go back to the Classic Maya period, and can be seen in surviving frescoes in Mayan ruins. The *marimba*, a type of xylophone, is the instrument most foreigners associate with the region, although it is thought to have been brought to Guatemala by African slaves. Many instruments were adopted from the Spanish, among them the *chirimía*, of Arabic origin, a sad-sounding wind instrument related to the oboe.

Ladino Culture

"What makes a Ladino?" has been the subject of public debate among intellectuals in the 1990s, as some Ladinos feel threatened by the resurgence of the Maya and by the international recognition of Mayan claims. In the 1990s, a Ladino is considered by both Maya and Ladinos themselves to be mixed race and part of the minority which has dominated the majority indigenous population in the economic, political, and social spheres. To be a Ladino means better access to health and education, jobs, the media, representation in the political system, as well as a higher standard of living.

Despite the diversity of Guatemalan culture, Ladino culture is what is taught to children in schools and predominates in the media. It is the result of conquest, as reflected in some of the most important national symbols. On the coat of arms, St Santiago gallops away on his horse against a blood red backdrop, while brandishing his sword and preparing to convert the heathens. Guatemala's original national anthem has so many references to blood and gore that in 1934 the government decided to tone it down and replace some of the references to "dyeing the flag in blood" and "torrents of blood" with flowery odes to peace. This is the version used today. Other than the Quetzal bird depicted on the Guatemalan flag, there is little in national symbolism to pay tribute to the Maya majority.

Many Ladinos identify themselves with their cuisine, which is a rich mixture of Spanish and Mayan influences. Guatemalan food is spicy and varied. One of the most popular dishes is *pepián*, a pungent sesame and pumpkin seed dish made with chicken and vegetables. Guatemalans are also proud of their *paches*, a tasty *tamale* made with potatoes as well as corn. The red light outside homes on a Saturday night in most *barrios* means that the *paches* are waiting to be sold.

The Maya celebrate November 1, the Catholic Day of the Dead, with modern versions of ancient feasts such as horse races in Todos Santos or kite-flying in Santiago Sacatepequez. Ladinos, after the traditional visit to the cemetery, return home to eat a special meal called *fiambre*. *Fiambre* takes days to prepare and is a cold salad of different kinds of meats, fish, chicken and vegetables. Families jealously guard their own recipes which have been handed down for generations. Guatemalans also prepare special drinks on holidays. Christmas is the time for *ponche*, a coconut and pineapple punch (depending on the family recipe), served hot. Rum is the national liquor, and the slightly sweet, dark and heavy *Ron Zacapa Centenario* is one of Central America's finest.

Ladinos observe other special holidays such as the *Huelga de Dolores*, a raucous Good Friday march through the streets of Guatemala City by university students. The 100-year-old march is a kind of political carnival and drunken free-for-all, and thousands of Guatemalans turn out to see

Huelga de Dolores, Guatemala City   *Paul Smith*

the students poke fun at the politicians of the day. The students take over downtown Guatemala City, clogging the main avenues with a procession of elaborate floats, and performing street theater en route. The party ends in front of the National Palace, the seat of power in Guatemala, where students spend hours hurling insults and sometimes vegetables and other items at the imposing building.

Going Global

While Maya and Ladino intellectuals clash in national newspapers in the 1990s about their respective cultures, the greatest threat to cultural diversity in Guatemala comes from globalization. Rap music, designer sneakers, television, and other influences are altering Mayan ways of life in rural villages faster than the Spanish conquerors ever dreamed possible. And while some Ladino parents may be anxious to promote their culture, making *fiambre* in November, and *ponche* at Christmas, their own children are barely distinguishable in their views and tastes in music, clothes, and food from many North American teenagers.

"The problem is that there is no exchange of cultures, just the imposition of American culture through television and all of the evangelical and fundamentalist religious sects that have invaded Guatemala in recent years. The goal of this cultural imposition is to create a market for *gringo* products among Guatemalan youth. The result is that young people, Maya, Ladino and Garífuno, do not identify with their own cultures. Since there is no state policy encouraging the promotion and protection of our national cultures, they end up choosing the easiest culture, the one that's imposed through the mass media. It's the imposition of rich America on poor America," claims Celso Lara, a Guatemalan sociologist.

Every October many Guatemalan children prepare for Hallowe'en just as anxiously as North American children, planning their costumes. In November, advertisements for turkeys and cranberry sauce abound in local newspapers, for those middle and upper class Guatemalan families who celebrate the all-American Thanksgiving holiday, or as they call it, *día de gracias*. Yet those same families have no idea when Mayan new year, the most important holiday of the year for Guatemala's indigenous majority, is celebrated, since it passes virtually unnoticed in the national media.

The cultural invasion is not only in the cities. Juan Manuel Sisay, an indigenous painter, belongs to the Tzutuhil ethnic group. Of all the ethnic groups in Guatemala, the Tzutuhiles are famed for aggressively resisting the Spanish conquest and protecting their cultural heritage. Tzutuhil men are among the few Mayan men in Guatemala who still wear traditional clothing. The Tzutuhiles also are famous for expelling the army from their town in 1990 following an army massacre. Not even the Guatemalan army could destroy the culture and pride of the Tzutuhiles, Sisay explained. But where the Spanish conquerors and Guatemalan army failed, television and the migration of many of their youth to the capital and the U.S. in search of jobs, is succeeding in turning people away from their community, customs, and language.

"Culture is a much more subtle and powerful enemy. Many people in Santiago have cable TV because the national stations do not reach our town. So young people, rather than listening to Tzutuhil music, prefer rap and heavy metal. They do not want to wear traditional clothing, they want designer sneakers and jeans. They don't want to speak Tzutuhil, only Spanish and English. They are ashamed of their culture. I am afraid that when our elders die, our culture will die with them, unless we do something to stop this trend."

WHERE TO GO, WHAT TO SEE

A magical way to enter Guatemala is by land, as the conqueror Pedro de Alvarado did. Drive from Chiapas, through the highlands, where the majority of the Maya live, into the departments of Huehuetenango, Quiché and Alta Verapaz. Buses are fine if you don't mind the odd chicken on your head and being crammed three to a seat in a very old school bus discarded by the U.S. This is the "backdoor" entrance, through Huehuetenango, the most ethnically diverse department in Guatemala, where seven languages are spoken. Local historians jokingly called Huehuetenango the backdoor to the country because during political upheavals, the *caudillo* of the period often fled to Mexico through this department.

Towering mountains — many active volcanoes, some still covered with pine forests, and others long bereft of trees — line the Pan-American highway, Central America's main thoroughfare. But tucked behind many of the mountains in valleys and ravines lie teeming townships belonging to the Mam ethnic group. Before the conquest, the Mam stronghold was Zaculeu, a collection of small pyramids just outside the now-modern town center.

The municipality of Todos Santos is well worth a visit, particularly on November 1, All Saints Day, when the locals hold an annual horse race, and the town is taken over by enthusiastic rum-drinkers, *marimba* players, and an increasing number of curious tourists. Todos Santos is in the Cuchumatanes mountains, on a dirt road which climbs to one of the most spectacular views in Central America.

One can enter the Quiché kingdom two ways, either by a beautiful dusty minor road to Sacapulas, or on the main road and through the chilly department of Quetzaltenango. Aguacatán lies on the minor road, a town where the women are known for weaving intricate hairbands that end in huge colored tassels.

The capital of the department of Quetzaltenango, also called Quetzaltenango, is named for Guatemala's nearly extinct national bird, the Quetzal. The Mayan name for the town, "Xelaju" (pronounced she-la-hu), inspired one of Guatemala's most loved *marimba* melodies, "Moon of Xelaju." Xelaju is redolent with history. It was here that the Quichés launched their all-out attack against Spanish conqueror Pedro de Alvarado, at first overwhelming the Spanish with some 30,000 fierce Quiché warriors. But their arrows and invocations were no match for the Spanish muskets

Santiago Atitlán and lake

Sean Sprague

and horses. Alvarado delivered a devastating moral blow to the Quiché here when he killed their leader Tecún Uman, who reportedly had gone into battle in a Quetzal feather cloak, giving Quetzaltenango its name.

The Quiché may have lost Xelaju to Alvarado in 1524, but today Guatemala's second largest city is commercially and politically dominated by the Maya. A Quiché Mayan was elected as mayor in the 1995 elections, and this small city has become an important rallying point for celebrating Mayan culture. The attractive town of cobbled streets and some of the country's oldest colonial architecture is also a mecca for foreigners who want to learn Spanish in some place other than the more touristy Antigua.

Back on the main road, the next stop is the capital city of Quiché, Santa Cruz del Quiché. This is where the Quiché had planned to trap de Alvarado, but he discovered the plot at the last minute and razed the town to the ground. The unrestored ruins of the former Quiché capital are just two miles outside of modern-day Santa Cruz. It is a sacred area used by local Mayan priests for ceremonies, as evidenced from the ashes, feathers, flowers, and wax left among the ruins.

Closer to Guatemala City on the Pan-American highway lie the restored ruins of Iximche. This was the former capital of the Kakchiqueles, where Alvarado established his first capital. Alvarado's bloody path across Mayan lands finally came to a halt in the eastern Kekchi territory then known as "Tuzulutlán," — the land of war — as the Spanish dubbed it. For those driving from Guatemala City, stop at the Biotopo del Quetzal, the government nature reserve where the country's last Quetzal birds still live, on the road to Cobán.

Cobán is a pleasant town, known for its excellent coffee and the continual drizzle that the Kekchi call *"el chipi chipi."* It is set in the rugged mountainous territory, covered with pine forests, that is known today as Alta Verapaz. It was here in the 1540s that the Spanish Dominican friar and human rights pioneer, Fray Bartolomé de las Casas, set out to convert the Kekchi Indians to Catholicism. He tried to convince the Spanish king, Carlos V, that more peaceful methods should be used to conquer the troublesome Kekchis, and that Alvarado's warfare should be replaced by the crusade of the cross. In 1547 Carlos V changed the name of Tuzulutlán to "Verapaz," meaning "the land of real peace."

Eco-tourists and nature lovers who visit Cobán should go to the famous Lanquín caves and the natural pools of Semuc Champey. There are organized river rafting trips in the department of Alta Verapaz, which is known for its strong and beautiful rivers.

After travelling through Mayan Guatemala, the Caribbean flavor of Livingston is an extraordinary change. Livingston can only be reached by boat from Puerto Barrios. The Garífuno are concentrated in the department of Izabal. This tropical Garífuno town moves to a reggae rhythm, with great places for dancing. It is located at the mouth of Guatemala's most beautiful river, the Rio Dulce. From Livingston one can take a small boat into a gorge where the river weaves between two rock faces that are more than a hundred yards tall. The rock walls that cradle the river are covered with vines and tropical vegetation that serve as a home to many birds. Not far up-river is a government nature reserve for the *manatee* or sea cow called the Biotopo de Chocón Machacas.

The far northern department of Petén is unique, famed for drug and wood smuggling because of its isolation. It retains its rainforest cover, where jaguars are said to roam, howler monkeys roar like lions, and Tucáns and Guacamaya birds fly. The tiny island capital, Flores, is the nearest town to the famous Mayan ruins of Tikal. One can easily fly to Petén from Guatemala City. By bus it can take between ten to fifteen hours depending on the state of the road, which is increasingly dangerous because of banditry.

Guatemala City is a modern, polluted, noisy mess of crime and contradictions, but for those interested in recent history and craft shopping, it is worth a visit to the old city center. The National Palace and the Cathedral are open to tourists. Behind the cathedral is the famous *Mercado Central* (Central Market), where careful shoppers who hang on to their wallets will find the best selection of crafts in the country. For nightlife there are two wonderful bars just off the plaza, the *Cien Puertas* and *El Portalito*. Che Guevara fans will want to visit this cantina which features nightly marimba music, huge glass goblets of beer, and was a favorite hangout of the Argentinian doctor during his stay in Guatemala.

Another historic bar in the capital is *El Granada*, also in the old part of the city. A huge old converted house with a garden, this has been and continues to be the nightly meeting place for now ex-guerrillas, poets, journalists, and a regular crowd who love the cheap *boquitas* (appetizers) and the conversation. This was the fateful spot where a young and drunken Jacobo Arbenz befriended the President of the Guatemalan Communist Party one night, and where the much-loved poet, Otto René Castillo, who was later murdered by the army, used to write his verses.

As any guidebook will advise, Antigua is a gorgeous colonial town with the best tourist infrastructure in the country. Another popular tourist spot is Lake Atitlán. For those who want to see the real Guatemala, avoid Panajachel, known disparagingly among Guatemalans as "Gringotenango" (gringo referring to white foreigners), and take a boat across the stunning volcanic lake to Santiago Atitlán. A short walk just on the edge of the town leads to the monument erected after the massacre in December 1990, where the Tzutuhiles changed Guatemalan history with their stand against militarization.

TIPS FOR TRAVELERS

Climate and Clothing

The coasts are hot and humid with a lot of rain, although humidity decreases marginally during the dry season (October-May). Everywhere in the country is damp in the wet season (June-September), with the rains making some roads and rivers impossible to use. Dry and rainy seasons are discernible on the Pacific coast and in the highlands, but the Caribbean coast is wet the year around. December and January are the coolest months, which, given the dry season, make them the most comfortable months to travel. In the evening, temperatures drop dramatically in the highlands. Dress codes vary widely, from smart Western gear for nightlife in Guatemala City, to tourist-casual in Antigua to traditional in highland villages. Anywhere off the beaten track in the rainy season is much easier with rubber boots, as unappealing as they may be.

Money

The national currency is the quetzal, named after the sacred bird. The exchange rate oscillates around Q6 to US$1. The best foreign currency to carry is the dollar and travelers' checks are the safest form. Both can be changed in banks and credit cards are accepted in Guatemala City and Antigua. Cash advances are possible in the capital.

Security

The political violence which has characterized Guatemala for decades has diminished dramatically, and never affected tourists much anyway. Since the peace accords were signed in 1996, however, violent crime has increased. It is always recommended that you look after your possessions carefully, and carry documents and money on your body. Petty theft and muggings have been common for some time, but what is new is the level of violence being used against both foreigners and Guatemalans in the course of theft. The lack of efficiency of the police means that in the late 1990s lynchings have increased, with citizens taking action into their own hands in an attempt to combat impunity. Tourists are generally not welcome to take photographs of people, religious ceremonies or children without permission. In particular, rumors that tourists kidnap children are rife, and it is best to avoid situations which might be construed in that way.

Women Travelers

The increase in physical assaults has affected women and caution is recommended. The *machista* culture does mean that comments and gestures are made by men on the streets at foreign women, but it is generally a nuisance rather than a threat. Nevertheless, a number of foreigners have been attacked and raped since 1996, many while traveling across the country.

Health

Although there is a potable water system that serves Guatemala City and some of the larger towns, bottled water is a good idea in order to avoid all-too-common stomach upsets. Most cooked food is quite safe, although you are taking some chances with street-stalls. But markets are plentiful and it is possible to eat fresh fruits and vegetables bought whole without adverse effect. There are no obligatory inoculations for Guatemala, although some are useful, such as typhoid and tetanus. The Petén and the Caribbean coast have high incidences of malaria and dengue fever, so it is good to go prepared. Pharmacies in Guatemala City and the larger towns do stock all the medication you might need. The most common complaint is diarrhea, which in most cases only requires drinking lots of water and occasionally body salts. Amoebic dysentery can be a problem, but a course of antibiotics will usually clear it up and these are available from local pharmacies. Guatemala City boasts plenty of doctors, most of whom expect payment at the time of the visit.

ADDRESSES AND CONTACTS

Embassy of Guatemala
2220 R Street NW
Washington D.C. 20008

Consulate of Guatemala in the United Kingdom
13 Fawcett Street
London SW10 9HN

The Guatemala Solidarity Network
26 Upper Tollington Park
London N4 3EL

Association of Artists for Guatemala
The Hideway, Hatford Down
Faringdon, Oxon SN7 8JH

Guatemala News and Information Bureau
PO Box 28594
Oakland, CA 94604

AmeriSpan Unlimited
PO Box 40007
Philadelphia PA 19106-0007
(volunteers and interns)

Journey Latin America
14-16 Devonshire Road
London W4 2RB
Tel. 44 (0)181 747 31 08

FURTHER READING AND BOOKSTORES

Many of the best texts on the country are published only in Spanish and are of limited availability. This list includes only books in English which are available in bookstores or good libraries. Excellent reports, analyses and other types of publications can be found in the documentation centers listed below.

Armon, J., Sieder, R. and Wilson, R. eds. "Negotiating Rights: The Guatemalan Peace Process." *Accord Issue 2.* London: Conciliation Resources, 1997.

Barry, T. *Guatemala: A Country Guide.* Albuquerque, 1995.

Black, George. *Garrison Guatemala.* Zed/Monthly Review, 1984.

Burgos-Debray, E. ed. *I...Rigoberta Menchú: An Indian Woman in Guatemala.* London: Verso, 1984.

Coe, M. *Breaking the Maya Code.* Thames & Hudson, 1992.

Colchester, M. and Lohmann, L. *The Struggle for Land and the Fate of the Forests.* Zed Books/WRM/The Ecologist, 1993.

Culbert, T. *The Lost Civilization: The Story of the Classic Maya.* Berkeley, 1974.

Dunkerley, J. *Power in the Isthmus: A Political History of Central America.* London: Verso, 1988.

Gage, T. *Travels in the New World.* University of Oklahoma Press, 1985.

Galeano, E. *Memory of Fire Trilogy.* New York: Norton and Company, 1998.

Gleijeses, P. *Shattered Hope: The Guatemalan Revolution and the United States 1944-1954.* Princeton, 1991.

Lovell, G. *Conquest and Survival in Colonial Guatemala.* McGill Queen's University Press, 1992.

McClintock, M. *The American Connection: State Terror and Popular Resistance in Guatemala.* Zed Books, 1985.

Montejo, V. *Testimony: Death of a Guatemalan Village.* Curbstone Press, 1987.

Painter, J. *Guatemala: False Hope, False Freedom.* CIIR and Latin American Bureau, 1987.

Schlesinger S. and Kinzer, S. *Bitter Fruit: The Untold Story of the American Coup in Guatemala.* Doubleday/Sinclair Browne, 1982.

Simon, J-M. *Guatemala: Eternal Spring, Eternal Tyranny.* Norton, UK and U.S., 1987.

Tedlock, B. *Time and the Highland Maya.* Alburquerque, 1992.

Wearne, P. *The Return of the Indian.* Latin America Bureau and Cassell, 1996.

Fiction

Asturias, M.A. *Men of Maize.* Verso, 1994.

El Señor Presidente. Aims Intl., 1990.

Goldman, F. *The Long Night of White Chickens.* Faber & Faber/Atlantic Monthly, 1993.

Perera, V. *Rites: A Guatemalan Boyhood.* Century, 1994.

Kee, C. and Norton, R. eds. *Guatemala: The Right to Dream.* Association of Artists for Guatemala, 1994.

Local Bookstores

Guatemala City
Sol y Luna,
12 Calle, 3-4
next to Bar Bodeguita, Zone 1

Librería El Pensativo,
7 Ave. and 13 Calle,
Edificio La Cúpula, Zone 1

Geminis,
Edificio Casa Alta,
3a Avenida 17-05, Zone 14.

Antigua Guatemala,
Casa Andinista,
4a Calle Oriente #5

Rainbow Reading Room and Café,
7a Avenida Sur and 6a Calle Poniente

Documentation centers

AVANCSO,
6 Avenida, near the corner of 4 Calle, Zone 1, Guatemala City.

FLACSO,
5 Avenida 6-23, Zone 9, Guatemala City.

CIRMA, 5 Calle Oriente,
No. 5, Antigua. (excellent library, particularly on indigenous issues).

FACTS AND FIGURES

GEOGRAPHY

Official name: República de Guatemala
Location: 15 30 N, 90 15 W, Central America, bordering the North Pacific Ocean, between El Salvador and Mexico and bordering the Caribbean Sea, between Honduras and Belize
Surface Area: 67,712 sq. mi. (108,890 sq. km)
Frontiers: 1,046 mi. (1,687 km) of land boundaries with four other countries: Belize 165 mi. (266 km), El Salvador 126 mi. (203 km), Honduras 159 mi. (256 km), Mexico 596 mi. (962 km), coastline: 248 mi. (400 km)
Administrative divisions: 22 departments
Capital: Guatemala City, population: 1,167,495 (1995 estimate)
Other Major Towns (1995 est.): Quezaltenango (103,631), Escuintla (69,532), Mazatenango (43,316), Retalhuleu (40,062), Puerto Barrios (39,379), Chiquimula (33,028), Antigua Guatemala (est. 30,000)
Infrastructure:
Railroads: 548 mi. (884 km), 63 mi. (102 km) privately owned; 548 mi. (884 km) single track
Highways: 7,460 mi. (12,033 km); 1,933 (3,117 km) paved (including 78 mi.

(125 km) of expressways), 5,528 mi. (8,916 km) unpaved (1996)
Pipelines: 170 mi. (275 km) for crude oil
Waterways: 161 mi. (260 km) navigable year round; additional 453 mi. (730 km) navigable during high-water season
Air Travel: 463 runways
Ports: Champerico, Puerto Barrios, Puerto Quetzal, San José, Santo Tomás de Castilla
Relief and landscape: Guatemala's physical geography is an aggregation

of mountainous highlands, forests, jungle plains, and volcanoes 2.36 miles (3.8 km) high. The Pacific coastline is an extension of Chiapas' Soconusco, replete with fruit, coffee, sugar, and cacao plantations. Black-sand beaches delineate the coastline, products of the sea's convergence with the volcanic slope. The western highlands are a continuation of Chiapas' Sierra Madre, a topography featuring pine forests, cornfields and 30 volcanoes (many of which

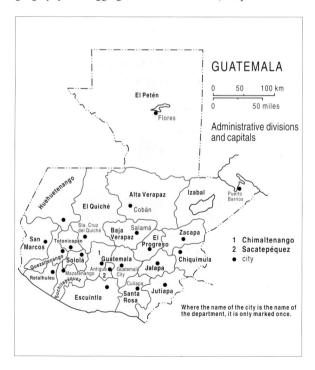

GUATEMALA

0   50   100 km
0   50 miles

Administrative divisions and capitals

1 Chimaltenango
2 Sacatepéquez
● city

Where the name of the city is the name of the department, it is only marked once.

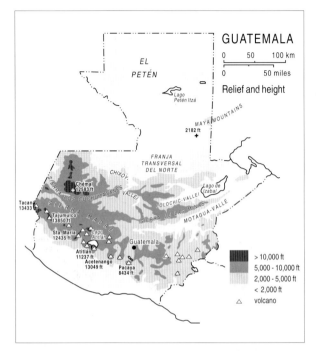

GUATEMALA

EL
PETÉN

Lago
Petén Itzá

0   50   100 km

0   50 miles

Relief and height

MAYA MOUNTAINS
2182 ft

FRANJA
TRANSVERSAL
DEL NORTE

CHIXOY

Chemal
12583 ft

Lago de
Izabal

Tacana
13433

SIERRA DE LOS CUCHUMATANES

VALLE

POLOCHIC-VALLEY

SIERRA DE LAS MINAS

MOTAGUA-VALLE

Tajumulco
13850 ft

Sta Maria
12435 ft

Lago
Atitlán

Guatemala

Atitlan
11237 ft
Acetenango
13049 ft

Pacaya
8434 ft

> 10,000 ft
5,000 - 10,000 ft
2,000 - 5,000 ft
< 2,000 ft
△ volcano

and December and January the coolest months.
Flora: more than 8,000 plant species in 19 ecosystems (including cloud forests at high altitude, pine forests in the mountains of the interior and mangrove forests on the coasts); approximately 600 orchid species, including the nearly-extinct white nun orchid which is the country's national flower.
Fauna: approximately 200 reptile and amphibian species (sea turtles, crocodiles), 250 mammal species (spider monkeys, pumas, jaguars, armadillos), 600 bird species (the national bird is the quetzal for which the unit of currency is named; also, parrots, toucans, macaws, woodpeckers, hawks, hummingbirds) and numerous insect species.
Environmental conservation and issues: 30 protected areas (including biological reserves and national parks) with another 40 in consideration for future protection; rapid deforestation of the El Petén jungle for cattle ranching and illegal timber harvesting is the most prominent environmental concern.

are active). At Guatemala City, the altitude declines to approximately 4,910 ft. (1,500 meters). The Alta Verapaz highlands north of the capital eventually yield to jungle in the El Petén lowlands, an extension of southern Yucatán. Southeast of El Petén is the banana-belt of Motagua Valley.
Climate: The coasts are hot and humid with profuse precipitation characteristic of tropical zones, although the humidity decreases

marginally in the dry season. Evening temperatures plummet in the highlands, with cool and damp days in the rainy season (June–September) and warm days in the dry one (October–May). Dry and rainy seasons are discernible in the highlands and the Pacific coast but rain falls throughout the year on the Caribbean coast. El Petén's climate is either hot and dry or hot and humid, with March and April the hottest

POPULATION

Population (1998 est.): 11,558,407
Annual population growth rate (1996 est.): 2.48%; at

this rate the population will double by the year 2021
Population density (1998 est.): 275 inhabitants per sq.

mi. (170 per sq. km)
Urbanization: 1998: 39%, 1994: 41%, 1960: 30%
Age structure (1996 est.): 0-

4 years: 17.0%, 5-14 years:
27.7%, 15-64 years: 51.8%,
65 years +: 3.4%
Fertility rate (1996 est.): 4.5
children born per woman
Infant mortality rate (1997
est.): 49 per 1000 live births
Average life expectancy
(1997 est.): 68.4 years
women: 63 years men
Public health care expenditure: 2.1% of GDP (1990)
Adult illiteracy (1995):
44.4%; women: 51.4%, men:
37.5%
Education (1991): 79% of
children aged 7-13 years are
enrolled in school
Public education expenditure: 1.6% of GDP, of which
65% was allocated to
primary and secondary
education (1993-94)
*UNDP Human Development
Index 1997*: ranked 117th of
175 countries (UK 10th, US 6th)
*UNDP Gender-Related
Development Index 1997*:
ranked 107th of 146
countries
Ethnic composition: Mestizo
(mixed indigenous-Spanish
ancestry) 56%, Indigenous
44% (census figures, see
text for more detail)
Languages: Spanish 60%,
various indigenous languages (including Quiché,
Kakchiquel, Kekchi) 40%
Religion: predominantly
Roman Catholic and Mayan
rites, but increasing
membership of Protestant
denominations, particularly
Pentecostal churches.

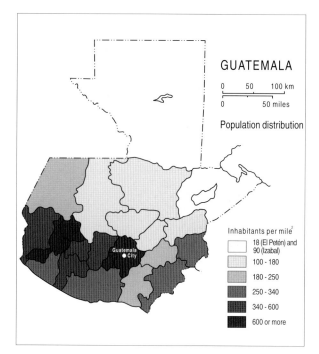

HISTORY AND POLITICS

Key historical dates:
* 1523: *conquistador* de
Alvarado subjugates
present-day Guatemala *
1676: University of San
Carlos founded in Guatemala City as Central
America's first university *
1821: Central America
proclaims independence
from Spain * 1822: Central
American region annexed to
Mexico * 1823: United
Provinces of Central
America declare independence from Mexico * 1826:
civil war erupts * 1839:
division of United Provinces
of Central America into
independent countries *

1859: government ratifies
treaty respecting British
dominion over Belize *
1871: Liberal reforms
introduced reducing the
power of the Catholic
Church * 1901: UFCO
establishes operations in the
country * 1898-1920:
Carbrera dictatorship *
1931-1944: Ubico military
regime represses unions and
leftist parties * 1945-1954:
democratic governments of
Arévalo and Arbenz
undertake social, constitutional and agrarian reforms
* 1954: CIA intervenes to
overthrow Arbenz in
"Operation Success"; land

reform terminated and political opponents killed * 1961: thwarted coup attempt by reformist military officers against conservative president Ydígoras * 1962: two guerrilla movements founded by coup conspirators; massive student and labor protests * 1963: suspends diplomatic relations with Britain and threatens war with Belize * 1966: thousands murdered by U.S. military-led counterinsurgency campaign and right-wing death squads * 1974: right-wing General Laugerud elected in fraudulent elections * 1975: EGP guerrilla initiates insurgency campaign * 1976: earthquake claims 22,000 lives; strike by workers at local Coca-Cola plant * 1978: union leaders assassinated; U.S. government proscribes arms sales to military * 1981: government refuses to acknowledge Belize's independence * 1982: guerrilla organizations and the Guatemalan Workers' Party form URNG; military dictator Ríos Montt introduces scorched-earth campaign in the countryside * 1984: year-long strike by Coca-Cola workers * 1985: Christian Democrat Cerezo elected president; U.S. government reinstates official economic and military aid * 1987: Central American peace accords begin * 1991: Jorge Serrano wins presidential elections; first official peace talks between URNG and government * 1992: indigenous activist Rigoberta Menchú awarded Nobel Peace Prize * 1993: abortive auto-coup by Serrano; former human rights ombudsman de León Carpio elected interim president by congress * 1996: conservative businessman Alvaro Arzú elected president; Final Peace Accord signed.

Constitution: Since 1986, presidential republic. President elected for five-year term (re-election prohibited) by universal suffrage (over 18 years of age); unicameral legislature with 80-seat congress; Supreme Court judges elected for five-year term by congress.

Head of State: President Alvaro Enrique Arzú Irigoyen (National Advancement Party/PAN), since 14 January 1996

Congress: number of congressional seats since 12 November 1995: National Advancement Party (PAN) 43, Guatemalan Republican Front (FRG) 21, New Guatemalan Democratic Front (FDNG) 6, Guatemalan Christian Democracy (DCG) 4, Nationalist Centrist Union (UCN) 3, Democratic Union (UD) 2, National Liberation Movement (MLN) 1; the DCG, UCN and UD comprise the National Alliance (AN).

Armed Forces (1996): total: 44,200. Army 42,000; navy 1,500 (including 650 marines), airforce 700; paramilitary forces 12,300; prior to the 1996 peace accords, approximately 300,000 were serving in civil Self Defense Patrols (PACs)

Military Expenditure (1995): $140 million, 1.4% of GDP

Membership in International Organizations: Central American Common Market, FAO, G-77, Inter-American Development Bank, International Labor Organization, International Monetary Fund, Interpol, Organization of American States, UN (MINUGUA), UNCTAD, UNESCO, WHO, World Trade Organization.

Media/Communications: 210,000 telephones (1993 est.); 91 AM/0 FM/ 15 shortwave radio stations, major stations (all broadcast from Guatemala City): La Voz de Guatemala (government), Radio Cultural TGN, Emisoras Unidas de Guatemala, La Voz de las Americas, Radio Cinco Sesenta, Radio Continental, Radio Nuevo Mundo, Radio Panamericana; 400,000 radios (1993 est.); 25 television stations, major stations (all broadcast from Guatemala City): Canal 3 Radio-Television Guatemala SA, Canal 5 Television Cultural y Educativo SA,

Tele Once, Televisiete SA, Trecevision SA; 475,000 televisions (1993 est.); major daily newspapers (all published in Guatemala

City): *Diario de Centro-america* (official), *El Gráfico, Impacto, Imparcial, La Hora, La Nación, La Tarde, Prensa Libre.*

ECONOMY

Currency: quetzal (Q); Q = US$1 1997: 6.10, 1996: 6.05, 1995: 5.81, 1994: 5.75, 1993: 5.64
Inflation (1997): 7.1%
Gross domestic product (GDP): 1997 est.: $17.4 billion, 1996: $15.7 billion, 1995: $14.6 billion, 1994: $13.0 billion, 1993: $11.4 billion
GDP per head (1996): $1,439
Real GDP growth: 1997 est.: 4.1%, 1996: 3.1%, 1995: 4.9%, 1994: 5.2%, 1993: 3.9%
Total External debt: 1997 est.: $3.4 billion, 1996 estimate: $3.4 billion, 1995: $3.3 billion, 1994: $3.1 billion, 1993: $2.9 billion
Debt-service ratio, paid: 1997: 14.1%, 1996: 11.4%, 1995: 10.6%, 1994: 11.0%, 1993: 13.2%
Poverty: 53.3% living on less than US$1/day (1989); 90% of indigenous people

living below the poverty line (1989)
Income distribution: Gini coefficient: 59.6 (1989); of national income, poorest 10% possess 0.6%, wealthiest 10% possess 46.6%
Economic aid: $1.9 billion pledged by the international community for ratification and implementation of the peace accords in 1996; Guatemala received $84 million ODA in 1993
GDP per economic sector (1996): agriculture 24.0%, commerce 24.6%, manufacturing 14%, transport and storage 7.8%, public administration 7.3%, private services 5.8%, other 16.5%
Employment: official unemployment (1994): 4.9%, estimated underemployment (1994): 30-40%; economically-active population (1994):

2,463,000; labor force (1994): agriculture 53%, manufacturing 13%, construction 6%, commerce 9%, services 7%.
Foreign Trade: Exports: total value (1996): $2,031 million; chief exports (1996): coffee $472 million, sugar $202 million, bananas $155 million, oil $60 million, cardamom $39 million. *Imports*: total value (1996): $3,146 million; chief imports (1996): raw materials and intermediate products $1,150 million, consumer goods $878 million, capital goods $691 million, fuel $330 million, building materials $95 million. *Principal trading partners* (1996): exports to: US 36.6%, El Salvador 12.7%, Honduras 6.9%, Costa Rica 4.9%; imports from: US 43.9%, Mexico 10.3%, El Salvador 4.1%, Japan 3.2%

GUATEMALA AND THE UNITED STATES/UNITED KINGDOM

Trade with the United States: exports to (1996): $743 million; imports from (1996): $1,381 million. Guatemalan foreign trade continues to be dominated by the United States. The US government has constantly intervened in Guatemalan affairs since the proclamation of the Monroe Doctrine in 1823. The United Fruit Company and the 1954 CIA coup are the most notorious illustrations. *U.S. Military Training*:

Guatemalan officers are trained at the U.S. Army School of the Americas (SOA) in Georgia. *U.S. Development Aid:* (1996): $69.9 million including military aid. *Trade with the United Kingdom*: exports to (January-November 1997): £14.7 million (1996): £19.6 million; imports from (January-November 1997): £31.3 million (1996): £27.9 million. Several international non-

governmental organizations (NGOs) based in the UK fund development projects in Guatemala. *UK Military Training*: The UK government provides technical assistance to the Guatemalan armed forces and police under the UK Military Training Assistance Scheme (UKMTAS). *UK Development Aid* (1996-97): £473,000 of which £48,000 was emergency aid.